St Augustine

PASTORAL THEOLOGIAN

Fernley-Hartley Lecture, Bristol, 1974

St Augustine

PASTORAL THEOLOGIAN

TREVOR ROWE

London EPWORTH PRESS

7162 0233 6

Enquiries should be addressed to
The Methodist Publishing House
The Book Room
Wellington Road
Wimbledon
London SW19 8EU
Printed in Great Britain by
The Garden City Press Limited
Letchworth, Hertfordshire SG6 1JS

TO FRANCES
auxilium sine quo non

ABBREVIATIONS

ACW   Ancient Christian Writers (London, 1946 f.)

ANCL   Ante-Nicene Christian Library (Edinburgh, 1867 f.)

Dods   The Works of Aurelius Augustine, ed. M. Dods (Edinburgh, 1871 f.)

LF   A Library of the Fathers (Oxford, 1839 f.)

Loeb   The Loeb Classical Library (London)

NPNF   A Select Library of the Nicene and Post-Nicene Fathers (Oxford, 1886 f.)

CC   Corpus Christianorum, Series Latina (Turnhout, 1953 f.)

CSEL   Corpus Scriptorum Ecclesiasticorum Latinorum (Vienna, 1866 f.)

PL   Patrologiae Cursus Completus, Series Latina, ed. J. P. Migne (Paris, 1841 f.)

ACKNOWLEDGEMENTS

Grateful acknowledgement is made to the following for permission to quote from works published by them :
Akademie-Verlag, Berlin (G. Florovsky, 'The Concept of Creation in St Athanasius' in *Studia Patristica* VI (Texte und Untersuchungen zur Geschichte de altchristlichen Literature, Bd. 81) Berlin 1962),
The Athlone Press of the University of London (N. H. Baynes, *Byzantine Studies and Other Essays*),
G. Bell and Sons, Ltd (K. S. Guthrie, *Plotinus, Complete Works*),
Cambridge University Press (A. H. Armstrong (ed.), *The Cambridge History of Later Greek and Early Medieval Philosophy*; R. A. Markus, *Saeculum: History and Society in the Theology of St Augustine*; J. E. B. Mayor, *Tertulliani Apologeticus*; D. Krook, *Three Traditions of Moral Thought*; H. Chadwick, *Origen: Contra Celsum*),
The Clarendon Press, Oxford (E. H. Gifford, *Eusebius: Preparation for the Gospel*; R. N. Flew, *The Idea of Perfection*),
T. and T. Clark, Ltd (K. Barth, *Church Dogmatics*, vol. III, Pt. I),
Doubleday and Co., Inc. (H. Pope, *St Augustine of Hippo*),
Epworth Press (J. Lawson, *The Biblical Theology of St Irenaeus*),
Faber and Faber Ltd (P. Brown, *Augustine of Hippo*; A. H. Hebert, *Liturgy and Society*),
Garnstone Press (Athanasius, *The Incarnation of the Word of God*),
Harvard University Press : William Heinemann (Loeb Classical Library, vols 193 and 239),
Hodder and Stoughton Ltd (J. Burnaby, *Amor Dei*),
Macmillan (M. de Unamuno, *The Tragic Sense of Life*),
Oxford University Press, New York (R. W. Battenhouse (ed.), *A Companion to the Study of St Augustine*; C. N. Cochrane, *Christianity and Classical Culture*; E. Frank, Philosophical *Understanding and Religious Truth*),

Palm Publishers Ltd, Canada (M. Pellegrino, *The True Priest*), The Paulist Press (*Ancient Christian Writers vols.* V, XV, XVI, XXVII), Penguin Books Ltd (T. J. J. Altizer and W. Hamilton, *Radical Theology and the Death of God*; D. Knowles (ed.) and H. Bettenson (tr.), *Augustine: City of God*), S.C.M. Press Ltd (C. Hartshorne, *Creative Synthesis and Philosophic Method*; J. H. S. Burleigh, *Augustine: Earlier Writings*; J. Burnaby, *Augustine: Later Works*; J. E. L. Oulton and H. Chadwick, *Alexandrian Christianity*; A. C. Outler, *Augustine: Confessions and Enchiridion*; J. Moltmann, *Theology of Hope*), Sheed and Ward Ltd (F. R. Hoare, *The Western Fathers*; E. Przywara, *An Augustine Synthesis*; F. Van Der Meer, *Augustine the Bishop*), The Society for Promoting Christian Knowledge (G. W. Butterworth, *Origen on First Principles*; H. J. Lawler and J. E. L. Oulton, *Eusebius: The Ecclesiastical History and the Martyrs of Palestine*; J. H. Srawley, *The Catechetical Oration of Gregory of Nyssa*; J. H. Srawley (ed.), *St Ambrose on the Sacraments and the Mysteries*; E. C. Whitaker, *Documents of the Baptismal Liturgy*), and the Editors of the following journals: *The Christian Scholar, The Downside Review, Mind, Pastoral Psychology, The Philosophical Review, Phronesis, The Review of Metaphysics, Studia Theologica.*

CONTENTS

PREFACE

A preface is customarily a vehicle for acknowledging one's debts and explaining one's limitations. I have good reason for wanting to use it for both these purposes.

Of my debts the first is to my subject himself. In his preface to the Basel edition of Augustine's works Erasmus described him as the Church's 'golden possession'. To me Augustine has been a constant source of enrichment over a period of twenty years. In the midst of a busy pastoral ministry, often overburdened in the way Augustine was himself, it has been good to find refreshment in this immense figure of Christian history. It was Dr Newton Flew who first encouraged me to explore the complexities of this great Father of the Church. I expect to be among the last of a long run of Fernley-Hartley lecturers to pay tribute to the stimulus Newton Flew gave to his students' researches. The encouragement and friendship of distinguished scholars has meant a great deal over the years. Among these stand out Professor Gordon Rupp, who first made historical theology exciting for me, Professor John Tinsley, who encouraged my interest to be disciplined by a research programme, the Revd Patrick Thompson, who supervised these early studies, and the Revd Gordon Wakefield, who encouraged me to write this book. My debts to the world of Augustine scholarship I have endeavoured to acknowledge faithfully in my footnotes. There is no way adequately to express gratitude for the help of friends, colleagues and students; nor to my wife, except by linking her name with the phrase Augustine used as a synonym for grace. In the preparation of the manuscript I am particularly grateful to the Revd Graham Slater, Research Fellow at this college, and the Revd John Stacey who have helped me to correct many errors and improve the presentation. Needless to say, I absolve all those mentioned from responsibility for the finished work.

When I was invited by the Trustees to deliver the Fernley-Hartley lecture at the Methodist Conference in 1974 I was engaged in an exacting ministry in the 'inner-ring' of Birmingham. There was little spare time available for preparation and I am grateful both for their invitation to deliver the lecture and their confidence that I should be able to get my material together in time. Since then I have been learning a new trade and resources of time and energy have been sparse. In spite of these restrictions I hope that the interaction between scholarship and pastoral ministry may have contributed something to this book.

I have concentrated upon the theological dimension of Augustine's pastoral ministry. Van Der Meer's magisterial book, *Augustine the Bishop*, is available to give an account of the practical features of his ministry. I confess that I have left to the reader a good deal of responsibility for making connections with current issues in the Church. It seemed best to err on the side of allowing Augustine to speak for himself.

TREVOR ROWE

The Queen's College
Birmingham

REFERENCES TO PRIMARY SOURCES

The following system has been applied: footnotes are in the form of an abbreviation of the title of the work and the book, chapter, section number, as required; after a semi-colon the volume, if necessary, and page number in the translation given below is printed. If other than the translation listed is used this is specified more fully.

Abbreviation	Title	Latin text	Translation
Ad Orosium	Ad Orosium contra Priscillianistas et Origenistas	PL 42	—
C. Acad.	Contra Academicos	CC 29	ACW 12
C. ep. q. v. Fun.	Contra epistulam Manichaei quam vocant Fundamenti	CSEL 25.1	NPNF 4
C. Faust.	Contra Faustum Manichaeum	CSEL 25.1	NPNF 4
Conf.	Confessiones	CSEL 33.1	LCC 7
De bapt.	De baptismo contra Donatistas	CSEL 51	NPNF 4
De bono conj.	De bono conjugali	CSEL 41	LF 22
De cat. rud.	De catechizandis rudibus	CC 46	LF 22
C.D.	De civitate Dei	CC 47–8	ed. D. Knowles, *Augustine: City of God* (Harmondsworth, 1973)
De corr. et gratia	De correptione et gratia	PL 44	NPNF 5
Ad Simpl.	De diversis quaestionibus ad Simplicianum	CC 44	LCC 6

Abbreviation	Title	Latin text	Translation
De div. qu. LXXXIII	De diversis quaestionibus LXXXIII	PL 40	—
De doct. chr.	De doctrina christiana	CC 32	tr. D. W. Robertson, Saint Augustine on Christian Doctrine (New York, 1958)
De Gen. ad litt.	De Genesi ad litteram	CSEL 28.1	—
De grat. Christi	De gratia Christi et peccato originali	CSEL 42	NPNF 5
De lib. arb.	De libero arbitrio	CC 29	LCC 6
De mag.	De magistro	CC 29	LCC 6
De mor. eccl.	De moribus ecclesiae et de moribus Manichaeorum	PL 32	NPNF 4
De musica	De musica	PL 32	—
De nat. boni	De natura boni	CSEL 25.2	LCC 6
De nat. et grat.	De natura et gratia	CSEL 60	NPNF 5
De nupt. et concup.	De nuptiis et concupiscentia	CSEL 42	NPNF 5
De opere monachorum	De opere monachorum	CSEL 41	LF 22
De peccat. merit. et remiss.	De peccatorum meritis et remissione	CSEL 60	NPNF 5
De serm. Dom.	De sermone Domini in monte	CC 35	ACW 5
De Trin.	De Trinitate	CC 50, 50a	LCC 8
De urbis excidio	De urbis excidio	CC 46	—
De utilitate credendi	De utilitate credendi	CSEL 25.1	LCC 6
De vera rel.	De vera religione	CC 32	LCC 6
De virginitate	De sancta virginitate	CSEL 41	LF 22

Abbreviation	Title	Latin text	Translation
Ench.	Enchiridion ad Laurentium	CC 46	LCC 7
En. in Ps.	Enarrationes in psalmos	CC 38–40	LF Psalms
Ep.	Epistolae	CSEL 34, 44, 57, 58	Dods Letters
Retr.	Retractiones	CSEL 36	—
Serm.	Sermones	PL 38–9, 1–50: CC 41	LF Sermons on the New Testament
Tr. in Jo. Ev.	Tractatus in Johannis Evangelium	CC 36	Dods, John

ANCIENT AUTHORS OTHER THAN AUGUSTINE

Abbreviation	Title	Translation
AMBROSE		
De myst.	De mysteriis	J. H. Srawley, *St Ambrose on the Sacrament and on the Mysteries* (London, 1950)
ARISTOTLE		
Rhetoric	Rhetoric	Loeb vol. 193
ATHANASIUS		
Contra Arianos	Tres orationes contra Arianos	*The Orations of St Athanasius.* The Ancient and Modern Library of Theological Literature (London, n.d.)
De incarn.	Oratio de incarnatione Verbi	*St Athanasius on the Incarnation*, ed. C.S.M.V. (London, 1953)
CLEMENT OF ALEXANDRIA		
Strom.	Stromata	LCC 2

Abbreviation	Title	Translation
CLEMENT OF ROME		
1 Clem.	First Epistle of Clement	LCC 1
CYRIL OF JERUSALEM		
Cat.	Catecheses	LF Cyril 2
CYPRIAN		
Ep.	Epistolae	LF Cyprian 3, part 2
EUSEBIUS		
Eccles. Hist.	Historia ecclesiastica	H. J. Lawler and J. E. L. Oulton, *Eusebius. The Ecclesiastical History and the Martyrs of Palestine* (London, 1927) vols. 1 and 2
Laus. Const.	Oratio de laudibus Constantini	NPNF 1
Praep. Ev.	Praeparatio evangelica	E. H. Gifford, *Eusebius Preparation for the Gospel* (Oxford, 1903)
GREGORY OF NYSSA		
Or. Cat.	Catechetical Oration	J. H. Srawley, *The Catechetical Oration of St Gregory of Nyssa* (London, 1917)
IRENAEUS		
Adv. Haer.	Adversus haereses	ANCL 5
Proof of the Apostolic Preaching	Proof of the Apostolic Preaching	ACW 16
JEROME		
Ep.	Epistolae	NPNF 6
Preface to	Preface to	NPNF 6

..

Abbreviation	*Title*	*Translation*
Commentary on Ezekiel	Commentary on Ezekiel	

LACTANTIUS

| Div. Inst. | Divinae institutiones | ANCL 21 |
| Epitome | Epitome | E. H. Blakeney, *Lactantius' Epitome of the Divine Institutes* (London, 1950) |

METHODIUS

| Symposium | Symposium | ACW 27 |

ORIGEN

| C. Cels. | Contra Celsum | H. Chadwick, *Origen. Contra Celsum* (Cambridge, 1953) |
| De Princ. | De principiis | G. W. Butterworth, *Origen on First Principles* (London, 1936) |

PELAGIUS

| Ep. ad Demetriadem | Epistola ad Demetriadem | — |

PLOTINUS

| Enneads | Enneads | K. S. Guthrie, *Plotinos, Complete Works* (London, 1918) |

POSSIDIUS

| Vita | Vita Augustini | F. R. Hoare, *The Western Fathers* (London, 1954) |

PRUDENTIUS

| C. Symmachum | Contra Symmachum | — |

2—SA * *

Abbreviation	Title	Translation
TERTULLIAN		
Apology	Apologeticum	J. E. B. Mayor, *Tertulliani Apologeticus* (Cambridge, 1917)
De orat.	De oratione	E. Evans, *Tertullian's Tract on Prayer* (London, 1953)
Adv. Marc.	Adversus Marcionem	ed. E. Evans, *Tertullian, Adversus Marcionem Bks. I–III* (Oxford, 1972)

Introduction

AUGUSTINE died in the year 430 AD as bishop of Hippo, a provincial town on the coast of North Africa—the modern Bone in Algeria. In spite of the greatness now accorded to him he was, in his time, little more than a parish priest. And yet, though there are things we do not know about him, he can be known by us more completely than almost any other person up to modern times. F. D. Maurice wrote of certain books 'which exhibit very transparently ... what sort of a person he was who wrote them, which show him to us. ... He may be writing about a great many things; but there is a man who writes; and when you get acquainted with that man, you get acquainted with the book. It is no more a collection of letters and leaves; it is a friend.'[1] Augustine's books are of this sort. To understand him we have to pay close attention to what he writes, but if we do not attempt, through the friendship of his books, to make the man our friend—and few writers give us greater help—we shall know about him, but understand him little.

Of all his writings the *Confessions* is most widely known. In that work Augustine quite deliberately exposed his inner world for all to see. Though this is his most obvious self-revealing work, the man is to be seen on all the other pages of his voluminous writings. Sometimes we are shown a man observing himself and the way he functions as a human being. At other times we have the intellectual struggling to find words and concepts to bring into coherence his understanding of Christian truth. We are shown the man interested in people and things happening around him. And all this is so clearly one man—a man who could not compartmentalize his experience—a man for whom life was a whole.

Augustine was born in 354 at Tagaste.[2] He was born into an aspiring lower middle-class family, which sacrificed in order to give him the sort of liberal education that might lead him into an honoured position in Roman society. Completing his

education, he became a teacher of rhetoric and, in 384, obtained
the important post of public orator in Milan. It was here that he
came into contact with Ambrose and here that he was converted
to Christian faith in 386. Two years later Augustine returned to
Africa and established a monastic community at his home town.
In 391 he was on a visit to Hippo when the aged bishop Valerius
called upon the congregation to choose a priest to assist him,
particularly in his preaching ministry. Possidius describes the
event : 'The Catholics were by now aware of the holy Augustine's
teaching and way of life and they seized hold of him—he was
standing in the congregation quite unconcerned and with no
idea of what was going to happen to him. (While a layman, as
he used to tell us, he used to keep away from churches where
the bishopric was vacant but only from these.) Holding him fast
they brought him, as their custom was, to the Bishop for
ordination, for they were unanimous in asking for this to be
done then and there. And while they were demanding this with
eager shouts, he was weeping copiously. . . . But they had their
way.'³ So began Augustine's association with Hippo. Five years
later, when Valerius died, he became and remained bishop until
his death.

Augustine did not begin his literary career on becoming a
bishop, but the major part of his writing falls into that period.
The question is sometimes raised as to what is meant by 'the
Patristic period' or 'the age of the Fathers'. As with most
questions the answer is not as easy to give as it may seem.⁴ In
general we can take it to mean that period in the life of the
Church when theological work took place in a pastoral setting.
It was bishops, not academics, who carried responsibility for the
exploration of Christian belief. There were those like Tertullian,
Clement of Alexandria, Origen and Jerome, who were not
bishops, but of these only the Alexandrians come close to being
academic theologians. In his early days as a Christian Augustine's writings mostly take the form of dialogues with his friends
or with himself. They have something of an abstract character.
This tone disappeared when he was given responsibility within
the teaching office of the Church. 'It was the needs and cares
of ordinary Christian folk that supplied both the matter and
manner of his loftiest writings, so that the main function of his

genius was to serve the pastor of souls.'[5] There is room for theology to work with great detail and draw upon the greatest scholarship that can be put to its service. Theology must address itself to a great variety of audiences—some sophisticated and others not. But always theology must be done within the dimensions created by pastoral situations. Augustine gives to us a paradigm of how this is done.

Augustine was a creative theologian in the sense that out of his existence as a man he was able to offer an understanding of Christian faith that brought together what was contained in the Bible and the Church's teaching and his own experience. He was not just a mirror reflecting the light that comes from the Christian tradition. He was the filament through which the Spirit flowed to produce new light.[6] Unamuno believed that the reconciliation of intellectual necessities with the necessities of the heart and the will is the basic problem men must face. Those who attempt it have what he calls a 'tragic sense of life'. 'There are people who appear to think only with the brain, or with whatever may be the specific thinking organ; while others think with all the body and all the soul, with the blood, with the marrow of the bones, with the belly, with the life.'[7] Such a man was Augustine. Not as exclusively for him as for Kierkegaard 'subjectivity is the truth',[8] for in Augustine there is a tension between the theologian and the champion of ecclesiastical order.[9] Nevertheless we cannot begin to understand him unless this personal dimension to his theology is recognized.[10] Was Augustine's doctrine of grace—the utter dependence of man on God—just the result of the challenge of Pelagius to what could be regarded as the orthodox Pauline view? It may well be that Augustine's view harmonized with that of St Paul, but also to be reckoned with are the evidences of strong influence from a dominating mother and a good deal of oral preoccupation—both of which may indicate the possibility of an unusually dependent streak in his personality.

The one obstacle to appreciating the creative nature of Augustine's theology is to regard him as a systematic writer. His mind had a poetical character. He was a master of rhetorical devices that give colour and vitality to his words, but these he was prepared to discard when, as tools, they did not serve his purpose. It is the function of poetry to bring together and hold in tension a variety of images that together evoke the truth. 'He does not do justice to Augustine who denies him inventiveness and free association, even if he must recognise that occasionally Augustine's syntheses were more neat than probable.'[12] The writings of Augustine belong to 'incarnational literature'[13] in which he permitted considerable ambiguity of expression in order to be faithful to a theology that centred in the Word made flesh.[14] 'Augustine is the greatest poet of Christian Antiquity, without ever having written any poetry worth mentioning.'[15]

Augustine was a contemporary theologian. By that I certainly do not mean that what is now being written as contemporary theology was anticipated by Augustine and that modern theology is a form of neo-Augustinianism. I use the word to emphasize that Augustine's work as a theologian was shaped by the issues of his day. He was a contemporary theologian in terms of the fourth and fifth centuries. The thing that he would have hated most would be Augustinianism, seen as an attempt to prolong the theology he forged for his day into succeeding centuries. These centuries were to present new issues to which new responses would be required. Theology is a hermeneutic process—a constant activity of interpreting the gospel to contemporary man. A theological system, which Augustine never sought to provide, or a series of theological responses, which he did, that seeks to have a currency beyond its time is dead. Theology is a living activity that seeks to repackage the gospel for each new generation and last year's wrappings will not do.

How, then, can the writing of the following pages be justified? Not long ago the paucity of books available in English on Augustine would have been sufficient reason. There was a serious gap in the historical resources upon which theologians must draw. In recent years some very fine books have appeared in this country—that will be noticed in the following pages—and internationally the output in Augustine studies is immense.[16] The relevance of this burst in writing seems to lie in two directions. First, one might look to Augustine for source material in discussion of a wide range of theological topics. This generation is not the first to have useful theological thoughts. Some new questions are being asked today, but mixed in with them are a

lot of old ones and the contemporary Christian might find help
from a particularly sensitive and skilful, if sometimes over-
ingenious, theologian. Industrialists are opening up disused mines
in the search for rare minerals today and it would be foolish if
theologians did not search for possible riches in a vein of theology
first worked in the fourth century. Second, one might look for
the resemblances between the problems of the fourth and fifth
centuries and those of our own day. Discussion of historical
parallels is a highly dangerous business and must be treated with
extreme care. One dominating concern for Augustine was the
unity of the church. But the Donatists were not like the Church
or Chapel down the road. The North African schism cannot be
compared exactly with any situation in our world today. To
follow Augustine's programme for dealing with schism would be
as impossible as it would be foolish. Yet, within Augustine's
teaching on the catholicity of the Church one can find shafts of
penetrating illumination as well as the source of many of our
ecclesiastical troubles. Similarly the fall of Rome was different
from the threats facing us today, but how a Christian responds
to the threat of change is of supreme importance for us.[17]

The subjects discussed in the following chapters have been
chosen to provide a cross-section of Augustine's thought as a
pastoral theologian. Many other topics could have been included.
Chapter 1, *On Spirituality*, is concerned with the heart of
Augustine: what is the nature of the Christian quest? Chapter
2, *On Preaching*, looks at that role which Augustine saw as part
of the pastoral office. It seeks to describe the character of
Augustine's own preaching and the guidance he offered to
preachers. Chapter 3, *On the Sacraments*, explores Augustine's
teaching on the sacraments, which was a source from which
derives so much of the ecclesiastical confusion with which
the Church currently wrestles. Chapter 4, *On Creation*, at one
level can be seen as merely descriptive of a complex exposition
of the Christian doctrine of creation. I include it because theology
like this was seen by Augustine as genuinely pastoral—it formed
part of the basis on which the Christian supported his faith.
Chapter 5, *On the City of God*, attempts to show how, in a
massive way, a theologian of genius ministered to his world in a
time of crisis.

NOTES

1 *The Friendship of Books and other lectures* (London, 1893) 4.
2 Undoubtedly the best biography is that of Peter Brown, *Augustine of Hippo* (London, 1967). A smaller introduction to his life and works is H. I. Marrou, *Augustine and his influence through the ages* (London, 1957); cf. also V. J. Bourke, *Augustine's Quest of Wisdom* (Milwaukee, 1945).
3 Vita Augustini 4; 198
4 cf. B. Altaner, *Patrology* (Edinburgh-London, 1960) 1f.
5 F. Van Der Meer, *Augustine the Bishop* (London, 1961) xvii
6 cf. J. E. Dittes, 'Continuities between the life and thought of Augustine' in *Journal for the Scientific Study of Religion*, Fall 1965, 130f.
7 Miguel de Unamuno, *The Tragic Sense of Life* (London, 1962) 33
8 *Concluding Unscientific Postscript* (Princeton, 1941) 187
9 cf. J. N. Figgis, *The Political Aspects of St. Augustine's 'City of God'* (London, 1921) 7
10 cf. J. V. L. Casserley, *The Christian in Philosophy* (London, 1949) 43f.
11 cf. Dittes, op. cit., 133
12 J. O'Meara, 'Augustine the Artist and the Aeneid' in *Melanges offerts à Mademoiselle Christine Mohrmann* (Utrecht/Anvers, 1963) 261
13 cf. E. J. Tinsley, 'Parable, Allegory and Mysticism' in *Vindications*, ed. A. Hanson (London, 1966) 175f.
14 cf. M. H. Carré, *Realists and Nominalists* (Oxford, 1946) 30 n2
15 Van Der Meer, op. cit., 567; cf. J. Searle, *Verses from St Augustine* (London, 1953)
16 cf. T. Van Bavel, *Répertoire Bibliographique de S. Augustin* (Steenbrugis, 1963) lists 5502 published studies and dissertations in the years 1950–60 and each year the 'Bulletin Augustinien' in *Revue des Etudes Augustiniennes* is a reminder of the continued growth of the subject.
17 cf. T. T. Rowe, 'Their Word to our Day II St Augustine of Hippo' in *Expository Times*, November 1968, 39f.

CHAPTER ONE

On Spirituality

WILLIAM HAMILTON described very vividly the stance adopted by many theological radicals: 'We concentrate our energy and passion on the specific, the concrete, the personal. We turn from the problems of faith to the reality of love. . . . We move to our neighbour, to the city and the world out of a sense of the loss of God.'[1] But it is not just radical theologians who adopt this style of life. A large number of Christians, without the sophistication of radical theologians, effectively belong among them. Part of my own experience is shared with them. It has contained two elements: the intellectual difficulties of theistic belief as it has been classically defined and a sense of unreality about a supranatural world. As a response to these elements I have found myself absorbed with questions about how love can be expressed to my neighbour, in the city and the world. This has not been my whole life, but a substantial stream within it over the past few years.

A pastor who finds himself in the position of sharing some of the experiences through which those for whom he has responsibility are passing is fortunate. He is able to understand and yet, through his theological expertise, can explore, for and with others, ranges of human experience that may be blotted out by certain characteristics of the modern scene. A pastor who lacks this element in contemporary experience has considerable difficulties; because he cannot easily imagine the experience he may find it difficult to listen at real depth to those who seek his help. He may give the impression that the problem being presented is a minor and temporary one, like a headache, and the best thing is to ignore it and it will go away. In caring for people in bereavement we know the damage that can be done when a bereaved person refuses fully to accept the death of a loved one. Similar damage can occur in the pastoral relationship when the pastor, by refusing to treat with due seriousness a sense of desolation, reinforces in the other a temptation to run away

from, rather than face and work through, the experience that has
come to him. I want to insist upon the pastoral responsibility to
treat seriously intellectual difficulties about theistic belief, experience of the unreality of a supranatural world and, not least, the
implications of the surge of Christian activism we have seen in
recent years.

How can this be approached? We must recognize that in
these three elements of contemporary Christian experience there
is a great deal of good. Belief, like so much else in human behaviour, can be imitative. That is, we can reproduce in ourselves
a pattern of belief that we have taken over without much
criticism from others. We can work on the basis of assumptions
that have a very shallow rational base. For people to have their
classical theistic beliefs challenged may be painful but beneficial.
For them to be called upon to re-examine the assumptions they
make about a supranatural world is healthy. To find Christians
moving into useful activity in the social and community fields,
becoming concerned about world development, facing moral
and political responsibility, is good in itself. What may help us,
is to see the interrelationships of these elements of experience.
People are made so that they tend to keep their intellectual,
emotional and behavioural values in balance—the homeostatic
or congruity principle.[2] When there is pressure on any one of
these we tend to adjust the others to restore the balance. So if
our theistic beliefs are disturbed our largely emotionally controlled assumptions about a supranatural world have to be
adjusted. In consequence of the loss, our behaviour must make
some appropriate response. If we work with the Christian triad
of faith, hope and love—that bears interesting relationships to
the triadic form of modern attitude theory—when we lose faith
we give new weightings to hope and love. Inadequate consideration has been given to the dynamics of changes in the form of
contemporary Christian experience and thus the responses of the
churches have served as a holding operation and not much more.
If a sense of the supranatural diminishes and thus worship, as
popularly understood, loses its point we give people things to
do. Stewardship campaigns, 'Fish' schemes, voluntary service,
all fine in many ways, have tended to confirm the new Christian

attitude-balance that has been struck. If God seems to die, we fill up the gap with humanity.

Augustine's approach
Is this the only way to proceed? Reformation of theistic beliefs is taking place and the literature is readily available. I am more concerned here with a series of other questions whose answers may make viable a Christian spirituality that takes into account aspects of human experience which may, at present, be in eclipse. I shall do so by asking how Augustine guided the development of Christian spirituality in times different from, but not altogether dissimilar to, our own.

Such a programme is fraught with many difficulties. So many of the aspects of Augustine's teaching that bear upon these issues have been the subjects of considerable discussion. Did Augustine distort the Christian tradition by importing an alien neo-platonic element into its spirituality? What was the nature of Augustine's mysticism? Where is Augustine to be placed in the stream of Christian teaching on perfection? What is the role of Christ in his understanding of spirituality? All these questions have been much discussed. I shall not add to the discussion except as it bears upon the limited issues with which I want to deal.

The Christian's goal
We must start by asking the fundamental question: What is a Christian? And, more particularly, the constituent question: What is the activity in which a Christian is engaged and to what goal is it directed? These are the questions an adequate pastoral theology must face.

It is to offer his personal answer to these questions that Augustine wrote *Confessions*. In that book we see a man moving away from a search for truth in the abstract to find it as something that absorbed his whole personality—reason, emotion, will.[3] Man's quest is not to be for intellectual enlightenment but for that 'knowledge which issues only out of the personal contact of life with life'.[4] For Augustine all human activity has to be directed towards the possession of God.[5] In the *City of God* he was to build his great description of history in terms of the different objects of human desire. But Augustine's preaching was full of references that indicate his awareness that men are directed by the objects of their love. 'What do you desire? I ask you . . . do not for the sake of reward love God; let him be the reward. Let your soul, say, "One thing have I desired of the Lord, that will I seek after; that I may dwell in the house of the Lord all the days of my life, that I may behold the beauty of the Lord." . . . Such will be that enjoyment of beauty that it will ever be present to you, and you shall never be satisfied; indeed you shall always be satisfied, and yet never satisfied.'[6]

Life, light and love

It is to the possession and enjoyment of God that Christ leads. 'This is the way; walk by humility that you may come to eternity. Christ-God is the country to which we go; Christ-Man is the way whereby we go.'[7] It is Christ who represents in himself the goal for the Christian man and the activity that will lead him to that goal. John Burnaby pointed out that the key words in John's Gospel, life, light and love, used to describe the revelation of God in Christ define the goal of Christian spirituality.[8] Man is intended to live, understand and love. All these three are diminished in him by sin. 'A life . . . which by voluntary defect falls away from him who made it . . . tends to nothingness.'[9] Thus the soul of man dies 'until it revives by the grace of Christ'.[10] Similarly man was intended to have his understanding illuminated by the inner Teacher.[11] But 'it is man's great misery, not to be with him, without whom man cannot be. Certainly man is never without him, in whom he is; yet if a man does not remember him, does not understand him, nor love him, he is not with him.'[12] For Augustine felt he could say on behalf of all men 'I know that I exist, I also know that I know . . . I am glad of these two facts.'[13] But he found his understanding diminished. Through grace God comes to live in man and brings the illumination that restores his happiness. 'Blessed are they with whom God dwells and who know it. It is this knowledge that is the fullest, truest, happiest.'[14] To the two goals of life and understanding must be added love, for 'it is as much man's nature to love love as to love being or knowledge'.[15] The restlessness of man is because his love is directed away from its proper object. 'You have made us for yourself and restless is our heart until it comes to rest in you.'[16] In fact man makes 'himself stoop unto earthly desires, he is bowed (*incurvatur*)'.[17] His love is directed towards his own concerns.[18] By the love of God shown to us in Christ man can be caught up into directing his desires aright. 'We could not have wherewithal to love him, unless we received it from him in his first loving us.'[19] Thus the proper goals for man—life, light and love—become the goals of the Christian man and are to be sought through the grace of Christ.

Happiness, peace and perfection
The process by which man's life, understanding and love are renewed by grace leads him towards happiness, peace and perfection. Happiness is not to be found in many things that men desire. 'As for riches and high rank, and all other things in which men who are strangers to true felicity imagine that happiness exists . . . they occasion, through our fear of losing them, more vexation than was caused by the strength of desire with which their possession was coveted.'[20] It is only as man is transformed by grace that he finds true happiness. In this happiness man gains peace in which there is 'nothing at all, in ourselves or any other . . . in conflict'.[21] In *City of God* XIX 13 Augustine gives a summary of the ideal of peace to which he sees the Christian life tending. It is an ideal in which not only the rebellion of man has ceased and he is no longer at odds with his creator's purpose, but a positive acceptance of harmonious relationships that fulfils God's intention.[22] All this is involved in the pursuit of perfection 'with the affections of the souls and the character of the life, so that they who possess righteousness may arrive at perfection, who, advancing in their renewal day by day along the straight path of faith, have by this time become perfect as travellers'.[23]

A corporate quest
It is clear that Augustine delighted both in solitude and the company of others. When one remembers the extent of his practical responsibilities it is certain that he must have burnt much midnight-oil in study and writing on his own. But he was obviously no recluse and had both a gift for friendship and a joy in the presence of ordinary people. So it is no surprise to find him speaking of a corporate quest towards the goals of

Christian living. On the one hand the quest binds men together. 'All men and all spirits who humbly seek the glory of God, not their own, and religiously follow him, belong to one fellowship.'[24] On the other hand they are aided in their quest by their social life. 'How could that City have made its first start, how could it have advanced along its course, how could it attain its appointed goal, if the life of the saints were not social?'[25] For Augustine no spirituality could be described without assuming the life of the Church in which individual pilgrims are sustained.[26]

Escapist?

If the goals to which Christian spirituality is directed are defined by God's intention for his whole creation then the quest must embrace every aspect of man's life within the created world. A spirituality that singles out certain aspects of man's life for development and excludes others will not do. So the question needs to be raised whether Augustine, in spite of his declared all-embracing goals, did in fact describe a style of Christian living that was escapist. Did he, as most of us do, point in one direction and walk in another?

Augustine has constantly been accused of advocating a world-denying asceticism. There is little doubt that he was dominated throughout his life by a 'search for the stable state'. A longing for permanence affected both his thinking and living.[27] He never seemed to come to terms with the transient nature of human experience. But alongside this there are other elements. Though he saw the impermanent world as something where he would rather not be—as it were a prison—he accepted this experience in a positive way. 'To one who rejoices, even a prison is wide.'[28] Friedrich Heiler has, perhaps, done more than most commentators to polarize discussion about Christian spirituality. So he quotes Augustine : 'If in me there dwells a desire for anything superfluous, do thou purify me, and make me capable of beholding thee.' Heiler declares that this indicates 'detachment from the feelings and desires of the self'—a characteristic of the purgative way—a component of mystical prayer that he opposes to prophetic prayer.[29] But Augustine commends a form of self-love. 'In some inexplicable way . . . whoever loves God, and not

himself, he it is that loves himself.'[30] It is when a man is absorbed
in self-love that he is corrupted. When he is so caught up in
God's love for him and begins to love in return he must love
himself—the object of God's love. All is superfluous until a man
beholds God and then nothing is. If he appears to detach himself it is in order that God's grace can rebuild his attachment.
Start from the assumption that every attack Augustine makes on
love of the world must be interpreted as world-denial and one
picture emerges. But if we assume, as Augustine gives us reason
to, that we cannot love the world until we love God then a quite
different picture emerges.

For Pelagius asceticism was one means available to combat
concupiscence.[31] Augustine had at the heart of his understanding
of the gospel the idea that it is grace that destroys concupiscence
and makes us free to live with joy in our Father's house. Far from
the Christian way being an escape it becomes the true way that
avoids the false trails. 'It is true that I love a certain kind of
light and sound and fragrance and food and embrace in loving
my God, who is the light and sound and fragrance and food and
embracement of my inner man . . . this is what I love when I
love my God.'[32] Here we see Augustine internalizing the love of
the world that arose from his love of God. This must be understood on the basis of the *uti/frui* (use/enjoy) distinction that he
developed in order to express his understanding of the nature of
love.

In 388 Augustine wrote that temporal things should be used
'as far as is required for the purposes and duties of life, with the
moderation of an employer instead of the ardour of a lover'.[33]
When a little later he wrote *De Doctrina Christiana Bk I* he
developed a much more comprehensive view. 'To enjoy something is to cling to it with love for its own sake. To use something,
however, is to employ it in obtaining that which you love, providing that it is worthy of love.'[34] Only God is worthy to be loved
for his own sake. 'We should use this world and not enjoy it . . .
so that by means of corporal and temporal things we may
comprehend the eternal and spiritual.'[35] When love of God is
placed first and the character of that love is seen to be described
so that all other loves must flow into it, then it is not only possible
but right to speak of loving the world in 'my inner man'.[36] As

Peter Brown points out, it is precisely Augustine's preoccupation with 'the problems of the relation between the inner and the outer life of a man' that makes him seem so close to us today.[37] When we polarize the two we indicate that we have not understood him. Undoubtedly Augustine does not offer Koestler's 'way of the commissar'—that organizes man's outer life—but neither can he be seen properly as describing the 'way of the yogi'—that reshapes man's inner life. What Augustine offers is a spirituality built on the model of the Word become flesh.

The imitation of Christ

This model did not immediately grasp Augustine's attention. At an early stage he seems to have seen Christ as 'the perfect example of philosophic detachment'.[38] 'I saw in our Lord Christ only a man of eminent wisdom to whom no other man could be compared—sent to set us an example of despising worldly things for the attainment of immortality.'[39] Later he penetrated 'the mystery contained in "the Word was made flesh" '[40] and saw the total character of Christ's life as a model for the Christian life. 'Whatever was done, therefore, in the crucifixion of Christ, his burial, his resurrection on the third day, his ascension into heaven, his being seated at the Father's right hand—all these things were done thus, that they might not only signify their mystical meanings, but also serve as a model for the Christian life which we lead here on the earth.'[41]

This patterning of the Christian life on the sequence death/resurrection/ascension was fundamental and needs to be emphasized so that we do not reduce Augustine's thought to a simple exemplarism. Certainly he made much of Christ as 'the perfect model of every virtue'[42] and indicates in great detail the obligations Christians have that are modelled for them in the style of life Christ adopted. But if this were all there was to it the Pelagian controversy would not have taken place. Pelagius gave great prominence to the ideal of *imitatio Christi*, quoting 1 John 2 :6, 'He that says he abides in him, ought himself also so to walk as he walked'—for the example of Christ is the norm of the Christian life.[43] Augustine parted from him at this point because he believed that Pelagius saw the Gospel as that by which 'we may learn how we ought to live; but not that we may be also assisted by his grace, in order to lead good lives'.[44]

Even when dwelling upon the human example of Christ, as given by God for us to imitate, it was the dying and rising of Christ that was the focus, and 'everything else he did' served as a commentary to make what was latent in these events explicit.[45] But the cross was not for Augustine exemplary—showing us 'the way to victory'—as it was for Pelagius.[46] When Augustine spoke of the Christian being renewed by imitating Christ's passion[47] he was referring to a theological world closed to Pelagius—a world which took seriously the Pauline view of man as a sinner, incapable of the imitation of Christ, except as his sinful self is destroyed by being crucified with Christ (Romans 6:6), and he begins to imitate the way of Christ at the other side of the act of grace.

Augustine understood the Pelagian scheme as dependent on the idea that sin continues in the human race after Adam 'by imitation'[48] and can therefore be removed by the imitation of the good. This was for Augustine in no way adequate to express the New Testament understanding of man or of his own experience. He saw the gospel offering man healing. And 'how can a thing be healed, if it is not wounded nor hurt, nor weakened and corrupted?'[49] In his pre-Pelagian controversy period Augustine tended to see the work of redemption, within man's temporal life, as the restoration of the innocence of Adam. 'There is ... a restoration of the inner man, when it is renewed after the image of its Creator.'[50] In this he lay close to the Greek Fathers in their concepts of recapitulation, apocatastasis and purification.[51] Later Augustine was to take more seriously the radical nature of the New Testament concept of 'new creation'.

There are images in the New Testament that support a return-to-the-beginning conception of the reformation of man, e.g. Adam and related allusions to the creation myths.[52] There are also suggestions of a reformation that is radically new. The idea of rebirth in St John may be shaped by the echoes of current Hellenistic literature in which newness is a moving forward into a new dimension not previously known.[53] On the other hand, it may be an image to contain an eschatological view of the transformation of man into forms of the glory to come.[54] Such an

interpretation would link with the eschatological element in St
Paul expressed most clearly in the metamorphosis image of 2
Corinthians 3 : 18 that calls to mind the Synoptic transfiguration
story which, in its turn, is filled with allusions to exodus—the
journey forward in which 'we are transfigured into (the Lord's)
likeness, from splendour to splendour'. Similarly Augustine saw
the reformation of man, not merely as a restoration of something
that had been lost, but as the movement forward to a quality
of life that had not been known, even in Adam before the Fall.

This is made clear in his complex discussions about the nature
of man's freedom. Free choice is found in all men, but freedom
(*libertas*) takes a number of forms. Adam possessed a freedom in
being able not to sin and this he lost in the Fall. The grace of
God is able to restore this freedom, but also Augustine looks
forward to a new level of freedom that will be a further act of
grace in which the Christian man will no longer be able to sin.
'The first liberty of the will was to be able not to sin, the last will
be much greater, not to be able to sin.'[55] Both these liberties come
to the Christian as gifts.[56] This view is finely expressed in the
magnificent closing passage of the *City of God.*[57]

The power of love

For Augustine the drawing power of love is crucial for the exercise of freedom. 'My weight is my love. By it I am carried
wherever I am carried. By your gift, we are enkindled and are
carried upward. We burn inwardly and move forward . . . we go
forward because we go up to the peace of Jerusalem.'[58] And the
love that gives freedom to our wills is kindled within us as we
participate in the dying and rising of Christ. An abundance of
texts could be quoted that express in a straightforward way the
connection between the love of God offered to men and the
cross. But Augustine's mind was not prosaic. 'He was funda-
mentally an artist. . . . The artist in Augustine felt free to com-
bine, to assimilate things that might seem to have no apparent
connection.'[59] So the very shape of the cross became for
Augustine a way of expounding the love that is seen in it.[60] In
contrast with Gregory of Nyssa he does not follow an interpretation that links the four dimensions of the cross with the
cosmic implications of redemption, but lets 'the breadth, length,

height and depth' be seen as aspects of love. 'The width of
charity . . . the length . . . is perseverance . . . the height . . . to
love for its own sake . . . the depth . . . we have not the power to
search through.'[61] The characteristics of God's love seen in the
cross are to be the marks of the Christian life.[62]

All this must be taken into account when Augustine speaks of
the imitation of Christ. Following the example of Christ's suffering is being caught up into love by the love of God. It is by this
'that we are renewed'.[63] Further ideas that express the radical
change in man that can only be brought about by grace include
hope that drives away despair[64] and the *Christus Redemptor*
theme.[65] The *Christus medicus*—Christ the physician—theme[66]
is of importance because it is linked with humility as a renewing
quality displayed in the whole life of Christ but seen most sharply
in the cross. Christ is the true physician inviting men to enjoy
true tranquillity when he says, 'Learn from me, for I am gentle
and humble in heart, and you will find rest for your souls'[67]—a
tranquillity that could not be found in the temple of Quies in
Rome. The enemy of man's peace is pride. This is a perverse
form of the imitation of God—'the soul prefers to imitate God
rather than to serve God'[68]—a failure in love's proper ordering.
'Thus the Wisdom of God, setting out to cure men, applied himself (as a bandage) to cure them, being at once the physician and
the medicine. Because man fell through pride, he applied
humility as a cure.'[68] 'Because pride had wounded us, humility
makes us whole. God came humbly, that from such great wound
of pride he might heal man.'[70] This is seen most sharply in
Christ's birth and death.

In a Christmas sermon Augustine gives vivid expression to
the humility[71] he sees depicted in Christ's birth : 'He so loved
us that for our sakes he, through whom time was made, was
made in time; and he, older by eternity than the world itself,
was younger in age than many of his servants in the world; he,
who made man, was made man; he was given existence by a
mother whom he brought into existence; he was carried in hands
which he formed; he nursed at breasts which he filled; he cried
like a babe in the manger in speechless infancy—this Word
without which human eloquence is speechless!'[72] Supremely it
is the cross in which the health-giving power of humility is active.

'On account of this great sin of pride, God came in humility. This mighty disease of souls, brought down the Almighty Physician from heaven, he humbled him even to the form of a servant, exposed him to despiteful treatment, hung him on the tree; that by the saving strength of so great medicine this swelling might be cured.'[73] Before such humility man's pride was exposed and so he turned to Christ as physician and cried: 'You shall heal me! I call upon you as being sick; I own you to be the physician.'[74] It is not that man sees what he is not and decides to choose another style of life—the physician gives humility: 'He who comes to me is made one body with me; he who comes to me becomes humble; he who adheres to me will be humble.'[75]

Identification with Christ is the whole dimension of the Christian life made possible by grace. It is spelled out in baptism and continues in the baptismal life that is nourished by the Eucharist. There is a secret life in which this identification is sustained, but we would miss a vital feature of Augustine's thought if we did not treat seriously the idea that healing comes in being made 'one body' with Christ.

The Church and spirituality

Earlier I drew attention to Augustine's emphasis on the corporate nature of the quest towards the goals of Christian living. This emphasis finds expression in the *imitatio Christi* theme. No doubt the setting up of a clerico-monastic establishment at Hippo owed much to Augustine's own strong need of friendship, but it is consistent with his whole attitude to the Christian life. He made it clear to the men who joined him that 'they were to imitate the mode of (his) life'.[76] But he clearly believed that the style of life he was offering was in continuity with apostolic imitation of Christ.[77] Basic was the communal element of the monastic life. The model taken was that of Acts 4:32. It was the attempt to live by this model that he used to justify his community of clerics to the people of Hippo.[78] It was also his starting point when he began to draw up rules for the nuns of his sister's convent.[79] When he wrote on certain matters that were disturbing the monasteries at Carthage, all that he advocated was built upon apostolic example.[80] Although Augustine was prepared to argue for celibacy as one form of the imitation of Christ, it was not a style of life that could be adopted by everyone and would be damaging to many.[81] It was not celibacy that made a monk but the endeavour to work out in community the imitation of Christ. To unravel the elements of Augustine's attitude to the clerico-monastic life would require a considerable excursus into a complex field. Involved in it are his own personal needs, the practicalities of organizing a controlled life for his clergy, a desire to create a new elite educated under his supervision for the North African Church, a substitute for martyrdom in days of temporal peace, and the fascination the ascetic tradition had for him. Sufficient be it to say that though he valued very highly the life he created for himself, his friends and colleagues, it was obviously not available to all. For most Christians the imitation of Christ had to be pursued within the normal corporate life of the church.

Christ and the church together form one organic unity. The individual Christian finds the life of Christ being created within him as he is part of the Body of Christ. Augustine interpreted 1 Corinthians 12 : 12 to mean that the members of Christ's body and Christ make 'the Body of Christ'—'The head and the body (are) one Christ.'[82] In another place he puts it paradoxically: 'Christ is still journeying whither he has gone before; for Christ went before us in the Head, Christ follows in the Body.'[82] Christ has not set us an example external to ourselves. The life of Christ set out in the New Testament does provide a norm of the quality and direction of the Christian life but as a living thing it is worked out in the corporate life of Christians in their time and situation. Preaching and pastoral care provide two of the means to this end, but chiefly it is the rehearsing of redemption in a particular time and place through the sacraments of baptism and eucharist, with their capacity for making connections with and between the varieties of human experience, that allows the life of Christ to flow in the church. The combination of sacraments, preaching and pastoral care saves the Christian from seeking a goal for his life apart from the grace of God.[83] 'Those who are fed like crying babies at the breast of the catholic church . . . are nourished . . . and arrive at last . . . to the maturity and hoary hairs of wisdom, when they may get life as they desire, and life in perfect happiness. Following after God is the desire of happiness; to reach God is happiness itself. We follow after God by loving him; we reach him, not by becoming entirely what he is, but in nearness to him . . . and in being inwardly illuminated and occupied by his truth and holiness.'[84]

What Augustine failed to do was to bring into congruence his concept of an unchanging God and a picture of man's spiritual quest in which both the grace of God and the freedom of man were equally active.[85] It may be, as Williams suggests, that a shift from Augustine's neoplatonic metaphysical assumptions to those of Whitehead may help to solve this problem. A search for theological coherence is important for pastoral theology because men cannot live happily with dissonance between their behaviour and feelings on the one hand and the cognitive levels of their lives on the other. What we can learn from Augustine is that no adequate spirituality can be built without carefully drawn objectives; that people need models on which to build a style of life—models rich enough to allow them freedom to respond creatively to the situations they meet; that no programme for the Christian life is adequate that does not take into account the whole of man's nature and that the corporate dimension within which man lives must be taken seriously. Augustine's solutions may not be correct for us—although I find them more fruitful than many alternatives I have been offered—but the way he indicates for building a spirituality cannot be ignored unless we are to submit too uncritically to the spirit of the times.

NOTES

1 T. J. J. Altizer and W. Hamilton, *Radical Theology and the Death of God* (London, 1965) 58f.
2 cf. C. A. Insko and J. Schopeler in *Attitudes and Behaviour*, ed. K. Thomas (London, 1971)
3 cf. R. L. Ottley, *Studies in the Confessions of St Augustine* (London, 1919) 88f.
4 H. S. Holland, *Lux Mundi*, 47, quoted Ottley, ibid.
5 cf. C. Boyer in *Spirituality through the Centuries*, ed. J. Walsh (London, n. d.) 15
6 Tr. in Jo. Ev. III 21; I 41
7 Serm. 123.3; II 522
8 J. Burnaby, *Amor Dei* (London, 1938) 147

9 De vera rel. xi 21; 235
10 De nat. et grat. xxiii 25; 130
11 cf. De mag. 40
12 De Trin. XIV 16; 114
13 C. D. XI 26; 460
14 Ep. 187.21; quoted R. N. Flew, *The Idea of Perfection* (Oxford, 1934) 196
15 Burnaby, op. cit., 160
16 Conf. I i 1; 31
17 En. in Ps. 50.15; II 380; cf. A. Nygren, *Agape and Eros* (London, 1953) 485
18 It does not seem necessary to contrast Luther and Augustine on this point as Nygren does. Luther specified the curvature in man as egocentricity—*incurvatum in se*—cf. E. G. Rupp, *The Righteousness of God* (London, 1953) 165—but for Augustine concupiscence was the effect of man's desires being directed towards himself rather than God.
19 De grat. Christi xxvi 27; 227
20 Ep. 130.3; II 144f.
21 C. D. XIX 27; 393
22 cf. Flew, op. cit., 205f.
23 De Peccat. merit. et remiss. II xiii 20; 53; cf. P. Pourrat, *Christian Spirituality* (London, 1922) 185f.
24 De cat. rud. xix 31; 222
25 C. D. XIX 5; 858
26 cf. Boyer, op. cit., 17
27 E. I. Watkin in *A Monument to St Augustine* (London, 1945) 106
28 En. in Ps. 141.19; VI 277
29 F. Heiler, *Prayer* (New York, 1958) 180
30 Tr. in Jo. Ev. CXXIII 5; II 543
31 cf. J. Ferguson, *Pelagius* (Cambridge, 1956) 136f.
32 Conf. X vi 8; 206; cf. K. E. Kirk, *The Vision of God* (London, 1931) 332f.
33 De mor. eccles. xxi 39; 53
34 De doct. chr. I iv 4; 9
35 ibid.
36 cf. De doct. chr. I xxii 20f.; 18f.; cf. Burnaby, op. cit., 104f.
37 Peter Brown, *Religion and Society in the Age of St Augustine* (London, 1972)
38 E. J. Tinsley in an unpublished paper *Augustine on the imitatio Christi.* In this whole section I am indebted to Professor

Tinsley's article and his willingness to allow me to draw from it.
39 Conf. VII xiv 25; 152
40 ibid.
41 Ench. xiv 53; 370/1
42 Pourrat, op. cit., 194
43 Ferguson, op. cit., 156; cf. J. N. D. Kelly, *Early Christian Doctrines* (London, 1958) 360
44 Ne nat. et grat. xl 47; 137
45 De utilitate credendi xv 33; 319
46 cf. Ferguson, op. cit., 131
47 En. in Ps. 36.27; II 93
48 De peccat. merit. et remiss. I ix 9; 18
49 De nat. et grat. xix 21; 127
50 C. Faust. xix 2; 318.
51 cf. G. B. Ladner, *The Idea of Reform* (Harvard, 1959) 153f. and also G. B. Ladner, 'St Augustine's Conception of the Reformation of Man after the Image of God' in *Augustinus Magister*, Communications I (Paris, 1954) 876f.
52 cf. T. T. Rowe, 'Comparative Study of Spirituality' in *The London Quarterly and Holborn Review*, January 1966, 15f.
53 cf. *Hermetica*, ed. W. Scott (Oxford, 1924) I 246
54 cf. C. H. Dodd, *The Interpretation of the Fourth Gospel* (Cambridge, 1953) 304
55 De corr. et gratia xii 33; 485
56 ibid. xii 34; 485
57 C. D. XXII 30; 1087f.; cf. E. Gilson, *The Christian Philosophy of St Augustine* (London, 1961) 323, n85; M. T. Clark, *Augustine, Philosopher of Freedom* (New York, 1958) 45f.
58 Conf. XIII ix 10; 304
59 O'Meara, op. cit. (Augustine the Artist), 252 and 255
60 cf. G. B. Ladner, 'St Gregory of Nyssa and St Augustine on the symbolism of the Cross' in *Late Classical and Medieval Studies in Honor of A. M. Friend*, ed. K. Weitzmann (Princeton, 1955) 88f.
61 Serm. 165.4–5; II 838f.; cf. also Serm. 53.15–16; I 58f.
62 ibid.; cf. Ep. 55.25; I 222f.
63 En. in Ps. 37.27; II 93
64 cf. R. B. Donna, *Despair and Hope. A study in Langland and Augustine* (Washington, 1948)
65 cf. P. Eigkenboom, 'Christus Redemptor in the Sermons of St Augustine' in *Melanges offerts à Mlle Christine Mohrmann* (Utrecht/Anvers, 1963)

66 cf. R. Arbesmann, 'Christ the Medicus humilis in St Augustine' in *Augustinus Magister*, Communications I (Paris, 1954) 623f.
67 Matt. 11:29 : C.D. IV 16; 155
68 De musica VI xiii 40; quoted D. D. Williams, *The Spirit and the Forms of Love* (London, 1968) 55
69 De doct. chr. I xii 13; 15
70 En. in Ps. 35.17; I 418–19.
71 cf. Serm. 184.1; ACW XV 71
72 Serm. 188.2; ACW XV 93
73 En. in Ps. 18 ii 15; I 139
74 En. in Ps. 42.7; II 207
75 Tr. in Jo. Ev. XXV 16; I 362
76 Serm. 355; Howe, op. cit., 207
77 1 Cor. 4:16; cf. Serm. 355; Howe, op. cit., 205
78 Serm. 355; quoted in Howe, op. cit., 206
79 Ep. 211.5; II 395
80 De opere monachorum; 470f.
81 De virginitate xxvii 27; 328
82 En. in Ps. 86.5; IV 218
83 cf. S. J. Grabowski, *The Church. An Introduction to the Theology of St Augustine* (St Louis, 1957) 13–21
84 De mor. eccl. x 17–xi 18; 46
85 cf. Williams, op. cit., 90f.

CHAPTER TWO

On Preaching

A U G U S T I N E , like Calvin, was one of the few leading figures
in Christian history, a large body of whose teaching has come
down to us in the form of transcripts of sermons. Though some
of his exegetical works were written deliberately as commentaries,
with a variety of purposes,[1] some have come to us in the form
of collected sermons. The works on the Psalms, the Gospel of
St John and the First Epistle of St John are of this sort.[2] Certain
writings appear in the editions of Augustine's works as treatises,
but were originally sermons preached on particular subjects, e.g.
De Continentia; *De Patientia*.[3] What are classified in the editions
as *Sermones* have been subjected to critical examination by G.
Morin and C. Lambot and their work, and that of others, has
vindicated the genuineness of about 500 sermons, published as
sermons, under Augustine's name.[4]

In Geneva John Calvin preached twice every Sunday and
once every day of alternate weeks. It is not so easy to determine
what was Augustine's practice in Hippo. It is clear that certain
sermons were delivered on successive days.[5] On other occasions
there is the hint that 'last Sunday's sermon' was the most recent
one heard in the basilica.[6] Two sermons on Psalm 89 were
preached on the same day.[7] Pellegrino's conclusion does not
cover all the evidence, but seems to give a general idea of
Augustine's frequency in preaching : 'Every Sunday, on the feast
days of the martyrs, Saturday and on the vigils of all feast
days.'[8]

As we shall see, there is plenty of evidence of the popular
enthusiasm that greeted Augustine's preaching. It would be easy
to conjure up the picture of avid listeners scribbling down the
words as they dropped from the preacher's lips and preserving
their notes, later to be collected together in a volume of *obiter
dicta*, like Luther's Table-talk. Augustine's energy was pro-
digious, but it is impossible to conceive his literary output
proceeding directly from the labour of writing. Though there

were members of the congregation who took down the sermons, or, as Possidius tells us, 'brought shorthand writers with them',[9] the chief burden seems to have fallen upon official reporters. Augustine apologized for a delay in writing to Marcellinus because he was overworking his amanuenses.[10] Evodius, Augustine's friend and fellow-bishop, spoke of his young 'clever stenographer'[11] and, in a letter to Aurelius of Carthage, Augustine assumes the availability of those who will transcribe certain sermons to be sent to him.[12] It is clear that his secretaries were constantly under pressure. On one occasion he wrote to Evodius that if he wanted answers to the questions he was asking he must send someone to copy certain of his writings, because he and his clerks were too busy to cope with Evodius' questions 'which are of interest to very few'.[13] Nevertheless their numbers were sufficient to record the sermons that the bishop preached, although the accuracy of their work seems to have varied considerably.[14]

AUGUSTINE THE PREACHER

Before we consider Augustine's theory of preaching and his attempt to apply the science of rhetoric to Christian oratory, we ought to attempt to catch the flavour of his own preaching. Possidius makes a high claim for Augustine's sermons. He believed that all who read Augustine's theological works would do so with profit. 'But I think that those were able to profit still more who could hear him speak in Church.'[15] Consider these two more modern descriptions. 'Very touching is the child-like simplicity, with which he gradually leads them through what to them were difficulties, watching all the while whether he made himself clear to them, keeping up their attention, pleased at their understanding, dreading their approbation, and leading them off from himself to some practical result. Very touching the tenderness with which he at times reproves, the allowance which he makes for human infirmities and for those in secular life, if they will not make their infirmities their boast, or in allowed duties and indulgences forget God.'[16] 'Through his genius for the right word he surpasses all the Church Fathers. Never once does he fail to make an idea unforgettable. Never once does he fail, when he desires to do so, to turn a simple statement into an aphorism. He never uses the sharpness of his mind to wound; on the contrary, every word he says carries its conviction by reason of an irresistible tenderness. Everyone who reads a number of his sermons will carry away the same impression as the men of his day, for no words from the pulpit have ever so fully come from the heart or combined that quality with such brilliance as did the words spoken by this one man in this remote corner of Africa.'[17] Such judgements are highly hagiographical and must be balanced by critical assessment, but they are not far wrong.

Confidence

For a man who could be consumed by anxiety over some things, Augustine gives the impression of being a confident preacher, despite the fact that he felt a tension between the responsibility laid on him to preach and the life of contemplation for which he longed. 'Nothing can be better, nothing more sweet for me than to gaze upon the Divine treasure without noise and hustle; this is what is sweet and good. To have to preach, to inveigh, to admonish, to edify, to feel responsible for every one of you—this is a great burden, a heavy weight upon me, a hard labour.'[18] His confidence is not surprising, for although there were certain aspects of his nature that disturbed him because of his inability to control them, his intellect was well under his control. He had no fear that he would not know what to say and how to say it. Speaking had long been his profession and for his skill in this field he was first called by Valerius to be a presbyter in Hippo. His confidence could not easily be disturbed. On one occasion he had prepared to preach on 'a short Psalm' but it seems that the reader was confused and chanted Psalm 139 with its 24 verses. Undaunted Augustine chose 'to follow the will of God in the reader's mistake' and proceeded to expound this Psalm.[19]

This confidence was rooted in role certainty. He knew what preaching was for, what he was preaching about and on whose behalf he spoke. It was for feeding the Lord's people and in the pulpit, seen as 'the Lord's Table . . . the minister ought not to defraud the guests'.[20] He sees the Christian congregation assembled for a banquet and his own responsibility to 'break bread'.[21] The preacher is present to give voice to the truth—and that truth of God given in the Scriptures. About this Augustine had no doubt and it was a well of confidence. Some passages give the impression of an undervaluing of the preacher's role—a view that is in sharp contrast with his practice. The reason for this impression is that he saw words as 'signs', the truth behind which could only be recognized as Christ, the inner teacher, teaches within. 'The sound of our words strikes the ear, but the Master is within. You must not think that anyone learns from a man. The noise of our voice can be no more than a prompting; if there is no teacher within, that noise of ours is useless . . . Outward teachings are but a kind of helps and promptings : the teacher of hearts has his chair in heaven.'[22] The preacher opens up the possibility for this to happen. In the end, as Hill puts it, 'God . . . only likes the sound of his own voice'—a reference to a passage in one of Augustine's sermons : 'The voice of God, from whatever instrument it sounds, is yet the voice of God; for nothing, save his voice, pleases his ears; for we also, when we speak, please him when he is himself speaking from us.'[24] 'Attend not to me,' Augustine says, 'the poor vessel, but to him who puts the bread in the vessel.'[25] This fact is a source of confidence as it accompanies a sense of high responsibility in preaching.

Burden and responsibility

As a bishop Augustine had been given responsibility for people and, though he found this a burden, he could not forget it. He was not his own master to do what he liked. After the fall of Rome, Christianity was attacked as a weakening force in the Empire. But Augustine could claim that in the churches people had learnt 'how they may so spend this earthly life as to merit a blessed eternity hereafter'.[26] He had kept faith with his responsibility. Though he loved solitude he needed people—he never saw the life of contemplation as being for him that of a solitary hermit, in spite of the influence of the story of St Anthony on him. He never saw ministry as being exercised except within a group-ministry—and he came to see his own salvation tied up with that of his people. 'Why do I preach? Why do I sit here upon the *cathedra*? What do I live for? For this one thing alone,

that we may one day live with Christ! This is my endeavour, my
honour, my fame, this is my joy and my treasured possession!
And if you have not heard me attentively, and I have for all
that not remained silent, then I have at least saved my own soul,
but I do not desire to attain everlasting salvation without you.'[27]
It was this sense of responsibility to people that led Augustine
sometimes to address his sermons directly to individuals within
his congregation, in a way that would seem quite improper
today.[28] While he was preaching on Psalm 62 an 'astrologer' was
pointed out to him in the congregation and so he went on:
'That thirst of the Church would fain drink up that man also
whom we see. . . . Having been led astray by the enemy . . . he is
penitent. . . . Guard him . . . in order that by your testimony it
may be proved to us that truly to the Lord he has been turned.'[29]

This sense of responsibility for people was made acute after
the fall of Rome when a sense of crisis was widespread.
'Augustine had . . . to make sense of suffering and political collapse on a scale that had taken his congregation by surprise.'[30]
So he spoke to his people in the familiar image of the olive-press.
'You look back to former times and these former times seem to
you to have been happier, which were like olives hanging on the
tree, swayed by the wind, enjoying their wandering desires like
a sort of liberty in the breeze. The time is come for the olive to
be put into the press. For they ought not always to hang on the
trees: now is the end of the year.'[31] In such a time 'Augustine
told them just what a demoralised group needs to hear. He gave
them a sense of identity; he told them where they belonged, to
what they must be loyal.'[32]

The preacher as expositor
All human affairs, ordinary or critical, could be interpreted by
the Bible. As an expositor of the Bible Augustine saw his chief
responsibility. So when Valerius gave to Augustine the responsibility of preaching, his first thought was to request a period of
leisure in which to further his study of the Bible. Writing to
Valerius he expressed his conviction that the study of the Bible
'is necessary for a man who ministers to a people in the divine
sacraments and word'.[33] He complains that time has not been
allowed to him. 'For what shall I answer to the Lord my Judge?

Shall I say, "I was not able to acquire the things of which I stood in need, because I was engrossed wholly with the affairs of the Church"?[34] The core of ministry is, as Pellegrino puts it, 'the ministry of the word and the Mystery of God'[35]—preaching, understood as exposition of the Bible, and sacraments. So Augustine saw the subjects for his sermons given, not by his latest idea, but by the lesson read from the Bible—a proper justification for preaching on a lectionary basis. 'The Holy Gospel which we heard just now as it was being read, has admonished touching the remission of sins. And on this subject must you be admonished now by my discourse. For we are ministers of the word, not our own word, but the word of our God and Lord.'[36]

Accountability and pride

For all this the preacher is accountable. He must himself be the hearer of his own sermon. 'We are ... bold to exhort you; and when we exhort you, to look into ourselves. For he is a vain preacher of the word of God without, who is not a hearer within.'[37] He must render an account of his own response to the word of God as he preaches it. The preacher stands too to give an account to God, in whose name he speaks: 'It is known to all, that of the bread which we have received, and which we expend, we shall have to give account.'[38] There is also a sense in which the preacher's faithfulness stands under the judgement of his congregation. 'I from this higher place advise, speak, preach: I denounce beforehand what evil must come upon drunkards. You have no ground for saying, "I have not heard", you have no ground for saying, "God requireth my soul of his hand, who never spoke to me".'[39] The congregation's responsibility is less than that of the preacher and Augustine often spoke of the danger in which the preacher stands: 'You stand in a safer place in hearing, than we in preaching.'[40]

Though the preacher may carry this heavy sense of responsibility, he is highly vulnerable to the temptation of pride as well as faithlessness. We shall see that the adulation of his congregation gave Augustine ample reason to know this danger. 'More happy are they that hear than they that speak. For he that learns is humble, but he that teaches labours that he be not proud, lest the inclination to please men to their hurt steal over him, lest he

displease God that would please men.'[41] In one sermon Augustine
pointed to Mary's sitting at the Lord's feet, hearing his words,
as a sign of humility: 'When we hear then, we are humble; but
when we preach, though we be not in danger through elation,
we are at least under restraint. And if I be not lifted up, I am
in danger of being lifted up.'[42] One has heard very many warn-
ings against pride addressed to preachers, but few indicate how
they have coped with popular acclaim. Van Der Meer gives us
a quotation from one of Augustine's sermons on the anniversary
of his consecration in which Augustine does this: 'I like applause
and it would be dishonest to say otherwise, but I do not want
praise from men who lead an evil life; that I hate and abominate.
It causes me pain instead of pleasure. But praise from decent
folk—if I were to say that I do not wish for that, you would,
I fear, think me a boaster rather than a righteous man. What,
then, am I to say? I do not altogether wish to have it nor to do
without it. I do not desire to have it, lest I be brought to fall
through human praise; I do not desire to be without it, because
I do not want to have an audience that is wholly unappreciative;
but I think of the burden of my responsibility, for I must render
an account even for your applause. Time and again I am praised,
but I am anxious about the manner of life of those who thus
praise me.'[43]

One way of preserving oneself from pride is the constant re-
membrance of one's debt. Augustine often brought to mind the
text of St Paul: 'What do you possess that was not given you?'[44]
So he spoke of his preaching as the paying of a debt[45] and gave
the best he had to give as simply as possible. We have already
referred to Augustine's sense of the burden of preaching—it was
the burden of this debt and he could not keep silent right up to
his last illness.[46] In this he deliberately followed Cyprian, whom
he so highly regarded: 'Ought the ministry of our heart and of
our tongue ever to fall silent in the few brief days of this life of
ours here on earth? Never!'[47]

Spontaneity
Augustine has certain obsessive traits, but these are not reflected
in his preaching. Spontaneity and improvisation were the marks
of his sermons. He was familiar with classical rhetoric which

sought to produce carefully constructed and polished speech, but
he pushed all this aside and saw communication as a relationship
between himself and his congregation that demanded a flexible
approach of a cybernetic kind—in which he could adjust his
presentation to the responses of his hearers. The appeal of his
message would not come through subtlety of presentation but
the conviction of the preacher. Augustine stated his extempore
approach : 'I shall tell you what the Lord may vouchsafe me.'[48]
He expected himself to be caught up in what God was giving
him to say and this would carry conviction to his hearers.[49] So
we see most of Augustine's sermons as improvisations on the
Biblical texts that had just been read. This explains the shortness
of the introductions to his sermons. He could not dwell at length
on what he was to say because he did not know where his exposition would lead. His introduction simply indicates the point
where he starts. In this he was following Aristotle, who spoke of
the *exordium* of a speech as 'paving the way for what follows'.[50]
Similarly he follows Aristotle's advice : 'Give the key-note and
then attach the main subject'[51] and to engage the attention of
the audience by emphasizing the importance of what is to be
said : 'Hearers pay most attention to things that are important,
that concern their own interests, that are astonishing, that are
agreeable; wherefore one should put the idea into their heads
that the speech deals with such subjects.'[52] It explains too the
digressions Augustine indulged in. Some of these were conscious
responses to something he had received back from his hearers.
Sometimes he responded, but unconsciously, as on the occasion
when he digressed, as he had not intended to do, on the errors
of the Manichaeans. He talked of this incident at table and said :
'I should not be surprised if the Lord was wanting some wanderer
from the flock to be taught and cured through my own forgetful-
ness and wandering.' A day or two later a man called Firmus, a
Manichaean, came to state that he had been converted during
the digression that had puzzled both Augustine and his fellow-
clergy.[53] But we cannot accept all the indications of spontaneity
and rejection of rhetoric at their face value. Augustine was a man
steeped in the skills of rhetoric—to whom they had become
second nature. When he came to offer advice to others about

preaching Augustine made clear that, though he rejected
sophistry, he saw the Ciceronian tradition of oratory as something
the preacher could not afford to ignore, as his own sermons
proved he himself did not.

Preparation

Though the text of Augustine's sermons was not prepared in
advance of delivery, much preparation preceeded taking his seat
on the *cathedra*. The most important preparation he refers to
in his handbook for preachers : 'Whether one is just now making
ready to speak before the people or before any other group or is
composing something to be spoken later before the people or to
be read by those who wish to do so or are able to do so, he should
pray that God may place a good speech in his mouth.'[54] Also :
'Praying for himself and those whom he is to address, he is a
petitioner before he is a speaker. When the hour in which he is
to speak approaches, before he begins to preach, he should raise
his thirsty soul to God in order that he may give forth what he
shall drink, or pour out what shall fill him.'[55] As this last quotation suggests, Augustine did, on some occasions, think out a
subject he wished to present in the form of a sermon. An
example of this seems to be provided in Sermon 21, on Matthew
12 : 32—the sin against the Holy Spirit. Augustine's decision to
preach on this subject was determined by the lection, but it is
clear that he presents a previously conceived treatment of the
subject. Indeed all his sermons proceeded from the long hours
of study and thought he devoted to puzzling over the Biblical
texts and the problems of Christian doctrine. In paying his debt
he made available all that he had received. There was no divorce
between his study and pulpit. So when, in a sermon, a problem
emerged to which he had not given enough thought he would
admit the fact and not attempt to muddle through. He asked
the congregation to hold the question raised in John 5 :22 in
their minds for the time being—'May the Lord himself then
follow with us, in case he may perhaps reveal himself somewhat
in these matters'.[56] In this case he does return to the question
later in the sermon,[57] but finally defers the matter : 'Hold me,
with the Lord's help, your debtor until tomorrow.'[58]

Relationship with the congregation

If Augustine saw that his congregation had a role in the preaching event, they recognized it too and did not hesitate to play their part. They brought to the basilica an enthusiasm that modern preachers might envy. From the very beginning of his preaching ministry Augustine attracted great crowds. 'With how great numbers are our churches filled, crowded up to the very wall; to what a degree do they annoy each other by the pressure, and almost choke each other by their overflowing numbers.'[59] They applauded when pleased, interrupted when they were confused and heckled if they disagreed. What a stimulating audience for a nimble-minded man! The people were nimble too: 'I see that you anticipate me by your crying out. For you know what I am about to say, you anticipate it by your crying out.'[60] Sometimes they were like children, as when Augustine told of a man, attacked by a lion, who strangled it. The people seem to have cried out 'Samson' before he 'mentioned Samson by name'.[61] This enthusiasm could sometimes be a nuisance. He had to appeal: 'You perceive that my voice is feeble; assist me by your calm attention.'[62] On another occasion he blamed, rather unfairly, the extended length of his sermon on the enthusiasm of the congregation: 'I have forgotten how long I have been speaking ... judging by this fug (as Hill translates 'odore'). I suppose I have held a long discourse: but it does not suffice for your zeal; you are too impetuous.'[63] He kept a rein on the responses of the congregation and did not allow them to give public applause to a view they denied by their private practice. When he was hitting out at the immorality of the theatre—as he often did—he raised great applause from members of his congregation who, in fact, attended the theatre themselves: 'What I want is good conduct. Let your praise of wisdom be in the manner of your lives and express it not through noise but through harmony—with the law of God.'[64] Similarly if they used the emotional power of the group experience to evade the demands of discipleship: 'It is easy to hear Christ, easy to praise the gospel, easy to applaud the preacher: but to endure unto the end, is peculiar to the sheep who hear the Shepherd's voice.'[65] How far Augustine recognized the greater danger inherent in this type of emotionally charged dialogue is open to question.

Peter Brown draws our attention to this: 'An audience will
identify itself only with an excited man: and Augustine would
be excited for them; vehement yearnings for peace, fear, and
guilt—these are the emotions to which Augustine's audience
reacted with shouts and groans. This could be dangerous. When
Augustine preached against Pelagianism, for instance, we can
see, only too clearly how Pelagius, the austere upholder of the
autonomy of the conscious mind, was outflanked by a man who
could put himself in touch with the more sinister currents of
feeling in a large crowd, with their pervasive sexual guilt, and
with their terror at the unsearchable ways of God.'[66] It is not to
Augustine's credit that he plays on sexual guilt, as when speaking
of concupiscence he says: 'Sometimes this concupiscence lies so
in wait against the Saints, as to do to them in their sleep, what
it cannot do when they are awake. Why have you all cried out
in acclamation, but that you all feel its truth? Modesty forbids
me to dwell upon it; but be not slow to pray thereupon to
God.'[67]

Though sometimes Augustine did manipulate, albeit unconsciously, his congregation, for the most part he attempted to
stand within it. 'This is the secret of Augustine's enormous power
as a preacher. He will make it his first concern to place himself
in the midst of his congregation, to appeal to their feelings for
him, to react with immense sensitivity to their emotions, and so,
as the sermon progressed to sweep them up into his own way of
thinking.'[68] Seated in his *cathedra* he would be able to meet the
eyes of his standing congregation at no great distance from him.
The sense of unity between himself and the congregation he
would reinforce by appeals for their cooperation and close attention. 'Pray for us, that the Lord may grant us to speak what is
suitable.'[69] One of his problems was the difficulty of convincing
his hearers across the clergy/laity line. The ordinary people were
inclined to regard their clergy as different from them—possessing
a sanctity to which they could not aspire. Particularly when
Augustine talked about sexuality—and perhaps with justice—the
tendency would be to write him off as a monk who lived among
monks and just did not know the problems they faced. So he had
to insist that bishops and clergy were not made holy by their
office. Much as the people would have liked a group of men on

whom to project their ideals, Augustine had to emphasize their common humanity. 'We beg that our debts may be forgiven us. For debtors we are, not in money, but in sins. You are saying possibly at this moment, And you too. We answer, Yes, we too. What, you Holy Bishops, are you debtors? Yes, we are debtors too. What you! My Lord. Be it far from you, do not yourself this wrong. I do myself no wrong, but I say the truth: we are debtors.'[70] When he was the subject of defamation for his former life, Augustine would not defend himself, but agreed with his accusers: 'We were deluded and infatuated in a perverse error, we do not deny it ... I am more severe to my own past misconduct than you are. What you revile, I have condemned.'[71] It is not the bishop in whom the congregation is called to trust: 'Christ is the gate of the city, he is not ashamed who stands in Christ and thus preaches.'[72] After all, how is the preacher to know who stands in his congregation to raise himself above them. 'I too was once where you now are; and I who am seen now to be measuring out to my fellowservants their food from this higher place, a few years since in a lower place was receiving food from my fellowservants. I am speaking now as a Bishop to laymen, but I know that in speaking to them I am speaking to many who some day will be Bishops also.'[73] This common bond with ordinary people held him firm—no fame or achievement was able to break it. Those who have been fortunate and have ministered to God's very little people will know the joy that is expressed in countless ways in Augustine's sermons and will not happily change their places to minister to God's very important people.

The close relationship between preacher and congregation we have described does not mean that Augustine was prevented from speaking, on occasions, very harshly to his congregation. In fact it was because this relationship existed that he, when necessary, could be direct without being pompous. These were his people—he was a father of these children—and any necessary chastisement disturbed him in the way known to all fathers. Usually the occasion for hard words was some problem of personal morality where the Christian position was clear—the people had heard it many times—but they continued to ignore it. We have already mentioned Augustine's problem in convincing the

congregation that the standards of Christian morality had to be
applied to all Christian and not just a clerical élite. On certain
matters responsibility took different forms on each side of the
clergy/laity line. Responsibility in sexual matters was one such
area and on this subject, in particular, Augustine felt required to
speak very directly.[74] On other subjects he could afford to be
more playful, if none-the-less direct; as when he chided a congregation for a poor collection: 'Now keep the poor in mind.
Give, you who have not given hitherto; believe me, you will not
lose it. . . . Now must we render to the poor the offerings of such
of you as have offered anything, and the amount which you
have is much less than your usual offerings. Shake off this sloth.'[75]
Augustine gives us his reasons for the direct, and sometimes hard,
tone of his words: 'In all my words I set a mirror before you.
Nor are they my words, I speak at the bidding of the Lord, by
whose terrors I refrain from keeping silence. For who would not
rather choose to keep silence, and not give account for you? But
now I have undertaken the burden, and I cannot, and I ought
not to shake it off my shoulders.'[76] He sees the words that he has
been given to speak as not being his possession to give if he will
—he is a steward: 'God bids, and I admonish because I am
admonished. He alarms me, who does not allow me to keep
silence. He exacts of me what he has given. For he has given it
to be laid out, not to be kept. And if I should keep it and hide
it, he says to me: You wicked and slothful servant.'[77] Never was
he prepared to acquiesce, in the realm of personal morality, with
the prevailing standards, if these were challenged by the Christian
faith. One point of interest, that we cannot delay on here, is why
this attitude did not always extend to political morality.[78]

Themes
The themes of Augustine's preaching cannot be summarized
adequately and briefly. He was, in the same sense as John
Wesley used the phrase about himself, '*homo unius libri*'.
Augustine's sermons were expositions of biblical passages—the
passages that had just been read in church. In these expositions
he called into service the whole Bible. Taking at random his
exposition of Psalm 64, we find that he quoted from 49 other
biblical texts. He had a view of the Bible that allowed him to

draw on passages to support others with little regard for their
historical context. This, which we would regard as irresponsible
today, should not make us miss the important point. What Peter
Brown calls 'Augustine's amazing power of integration'[79] was seen
in his biblical exposition : 'Each Psalm . . . could be presented as a
microcosm of the whole Bible—the clear essence of Christianity
refracted in the exotic spectrum of a Hebrew poem.'[80] It is to
be seen in all his preaching. He did not reserve one set of
thoughts for his treatises and another for his sermons. When he
preached on St John's Gospel he would not give less than his
best, attempting patiently to lead his congregation into the deep
questions that puzzled him. All the time he was seeking to draw
his congregation into a unity of understanding, both among
themselves and also with the whole catholic Church. To do this
he had to clarify and integrate the Church's teaching. Having
sung Psalm 19 Augustine said to the people : 'Therefore, dearest
brethren, what we have sung with accordant voice, we ought
also with an understanding heart to know and understand.'[81]
He then went on to expound the Psalm so that the people could
move from a united voice to a united mind. Augustine was
concerned too to direct his people to the single source of Christian
experience around which to build their unity : Christ. In his
sermons he called his people to respond to the love of God in
Christ with their own love and devotion. For, as he was to
explain more fully in *De civitate Dei*, on this love is founded the
City of God. 'Men who love one another, and who love their
God who dwells in them, constitute a city unto God. He therefore
who is full of love, is full of God. . . . Be in it and God shall not
be apart from you.'[82] Another form of unity into which Augustine
sought to draw his congregation was a common style of Christian
discipleship. The Bible was a storehouse of practical divinity and
Christian doctrine in the patristic period was pastoral rather than
academic in its motivation. Augustine knew the temptations
that came to people in their day-to-day lives and so he would
call them to be on their guard : 'Let the hand do nothing wrong,
let the feet run not to any evil, nor the eye be directed to
immodesty; let not the ear be open with pleasure to filthy talk;
nor the tongue move to indecent speech.'[83] When dealing with
the habit of swearing he proposed a three-day cure. He told

them : when you get home and 'by a slip of the tongue . . . have
repeated the habit; let neighbour admonish neighbour : "This
is what we heard today, this is what we are bound to". Let it
(the swearing) not be done today, at all events when the sermon
is fresh. I speak from experience; let it not be done today, it is
less readily done tomorrow. If tomorrow too it shall not be done,
less is the labour of him who is on his guard for he is helped by
the custom of the day before. The third day the plague, by
which we suffer, dies.'[84] He would emphasize also the Christian's
responsibility for witnessing to his faith : 'Preach wherever you
can, to whom you can and as you can.'[85] One sermon, that
illustrates both the practical orientation of Augustine's preaching
and the subtlety of his presentation, was addressed to businessmen
and based on Psalm 71 : 15 : 'My mouth shall declare your
salvation . . . I have not known businesses' (in Augustine's version
of the Psalter). 'It is high time Christians mended their ways—
they must give up their businesses. But then the business man
says to me "Look here, I bring my goods a long distance to places
where they could not otherwise be had, that is how I earn my
living. . . . You are on about lying and perjury. Well that is my
fault, not the business's. It is not as if I could not carry on
business without this. I am not going to bring an action against
my business, and blame it for what is my own fault. If I tell a
lie, then *I* lie, not the business." That is what the business man
would say to me. "Well, Bishop, you must find some other way
of understanding what is meant by these businesses you have
read about in your psalter; else *you* will fail to understand, and
I will be denied the right to my business. By all means admonish
me on how I ought to live; it will do me good if you do it well.
One thing I am certain of—if I am bad, it is not my business
but my own wickedness that makes me so." Well, when someone
states the truth like that there is no gainsaying it.'[86]

Illustrations
All the subjects Augustine treated were enlightened by a constant
stream of lively, imaginative and humorous illustrations. It is
almost impossible to believe that so distinguished an Augustine
scholar as J. H. S. Burleigh could write of 'the absence of illustrations from life' in Augustine's sermons.[87] One of the most im-

pressive features of Augustine's preaching is the way in which
his imagination catches unusual forms of expression and how he
draws into his service striking metaphors. He does indulge in
much play on words that is mostly lost in translation and would
probably not be appreciated by a modern audience—but it
seemed to delight the North Africans. It is not difficult to imagine
the way in which some of his more fanciful ideas helped a truth
to stick in the mind. For example, Augustine made the point
that Adam represented the whole human race by pointing to
the fact that the first letter of the Greek words for East, West,
North and South made up the word ADAM.[88] Or who could
forget his statement about the avarice of the rich : 'You believe
that they are satisfied? Far from it! They no longer desire to
drink from a beaker because they thirst after the whole river.'[89]
Augustine could tell stories succinctly, such as that of the man
he had known in Milan who found some money, 'if the number
does not escape me ... about 200 shillings', and first refused to
accept and finally determined to keep the reward offered.[90] This
story he made into another method of admonishing his congregation to be free of avarice. Augustine's humour could come spilling
out in vivid images : 'What is so uncertain as a rolling thing?
It is not unfitly that money itself is stamped round, because it
remains not still.'[91] His illustrations were not used simply to
entertain, but to enliven what was being said so that the point
being illustrated would catch the attention of his hearers. He
remained throughout a servant of the Word.

Though Augustine brought great natural skills to the preaching art, it is clear that he put great value upon the necessary
hard work required of a successful preacher. The preacher has
to work for lucidity. 'Let those rage against you who know not
with what sighs and groans the least particle of the knowledge
of God is obtained.'[92] Not the least part of this labour has to
be expended in the preacher adapting himself to the level at
which the congregation can make a response. On certain occasions Augustine made great demands upon his congregation, but
he took pains to meet them at their level of understanding. He
was capable of great eloquence, by the standards of the rhetoricians, but this he was prepared to put aside in the cause of effective
communication. 'What matters it to us, what the grammarians

please to rule? It were better for us to be guilty of a barbarism,
so that you understand, than that in our propriety of speech you
are left unprovided.'[93] He neither ignored the educational
deficiencies of his congregation nor was paternalistic towards
them. They made up one facet in the relationship between
preacher and congregation and controlled his speech as did many
other factors; for example, his own self-confessed feeble voice.
Though not short of ideas, Augustine would repeat himself, as he
explains in *De catechizandis rudibus*,[94] for his congregation's sake.
He was far from insensitive to the strain he sometimes put on
his listeners. On one occasion he broke off his exposition of a
Psalm so that people could go out for a meal and return for
the second part of the sermon—a confident preacher indeed!
'Let us, if you please, reserve what remains; since the Psalm is a
long one, and we have yet some further opportunity of speaking
with you in Christ's name. Refresh your strength therefore : I
do not mean that of your mind, for in mind I see you are incapable of fatigue; but on account of the slaves of the soul, that
your bodies may be sustained in their service, refresh yourselves
for a little, and being refreshed return to your meal.'[95] The same
level of sensitivity to his hearers could have made him able to
manipulate the needs and fears of his congregation. Fear of Hell
was not far from the people's minds at that time, but in one
sermon, while he recognized this fear he did not play on it—he
accepted it and then nicely displaced it by asking his congregation to regard Hell, not so much as a place of physical torment,
but where they would be deprived of the ones they love.[96]
Augustine was a master at recognizing the 'latitude of acceptance'
in his congregation, that we have come to recognize as being
essential in securing a change of attitude.[97]

It is difficult to decide what level of seriousness Augustine
brought to one feature of his biblical exegesis. There is a
theatrical quality about some of his allegorical exegesis and his
clear fascination with numerical images. Was this because he
recognized the needs of his congregation for entertainment as
well as enlightenment? Or do we see these passages as entertain-
ing because we do not approach this style of interpretation with
seriousness? One passage seems to indicate that the preacher
and the congregation came to these expositions from different

angles : Augustine as an expositor of scripture and the people as those who had become familiar with allegory in the theatres. 'Many things seem to have one sound and another meaning, and that is called allegory. For he that thinks I said allegory with reference to the theatre, let him think that the Lord also spoke "Parabola" of the amphitheatre. You see what comes of a city where shows abound ! I should speak more safely in the country; for there men would not have learned what allegory is, save in the Scriptures of God.'[98] Nevertheless the people enjoyed the way in which Augustine made the Bible into a gigantic puzzle[99] and constantly succeeded in unravelling it for them.[100]

AUGUSTINE THE TEACHER OF PREACHERS

These are some of the features of Augustine's preaching that can be deduced from the transcripts of his sermons. What Augustine has also given to us is a treatment of rhetoric for the preacher in *De doctrina Christiana Book IV* and an introduction to catechesis in *De catechizandis rudibus*.

On catechizing

Though *De catechizandis rudibus* was written with the particular problems of Deogratias of Carthage, as a catechist, in view, some of the things Augustine has to say are of importance to preachers. Preaching is a particular form of human relationship. If this relationship is to be effective, the two ends of the communication process must be given consideration—the transmitter and the receiver—the preacher and the congregation. Augustine drew the attention of Deogratias to certain characteristics of different kinds of people who would present themselves for instruction. Not to take these characteristics into consideration would lead to a breakdown of communication. Similarly there are certain characteristics that a good communicator must possess or acquire. Augustine recognized the great difference between private and public speaking. In private one has a single target audience whose characteristics can be assessed with some accuracy. In public one cannot know precisely the characteristics of one's audience. 'It is different when one is admonishing

privately, with no other person near to form a judgement of us,
from that, when one is teaching openly, surrounded by an
auditory of persons who hold very different opinions . . . it makes
much difference also, when we are thus speaking, whether there
be few present or many, learned or unlearned, or made up of
both; citizens or rustics, or both together, or again a people
mingled of all classes. For it cannot be, but that they affect in
different ways the man who has to speak and address them, and
that both the discourse which is delivered carries as it were a
certain stamp of feature expressive of the feeling of the mind
from which it issues, and according to this same difference affects
the hearers in different ways, they give in their turn by their
very presence affecting each other in different ways.'[101] Here
Augustine has recognized those elements that are being explored
in modern communication theory, in particular the limited
capacity of hearers, the assumptions a communicator makes that
will be read differently by individual hearers, the conscious and
unconscious mechanisms by which, through projection, identification or repression, the receiver hears something different from
his neighbour.[102] He was also seeing that the dynamics of the
preaching relationship include intra-congregational relationships
as well as the preacher/congregation relationship. Augustine
seems to have understood well, with Aristotle, that 'every speech
is composed of three parts: the speaker, the subject of which he
treats, and the person to whom it is addressed',[103] and that of
these three the audience is primary in importance.

Augustine did not engage in the close analysis of the particular
emotional characteristics of the audience that Aristotle did in
Rhetoric Book II, but in *De catechizandis rudibus*, and in his
own practice as a preacher, we find recognition of this factor.
'All have a claim on us for the same love, yet it is not the same
medicine to be used for all; so love itself in like manner is in
travail with some, is made weak together with others, some it
seeks to edify, to others it carries itself erect, to some it is gentle,
to others severe, to none as an enemy, to all as a mother.'[104]
Augustine described from his own experience some of those who
come for instruction and what approach is appropriate to them,
e.g. the educated man,[105] the half-educated,[106] people who want
to benefit from the respectability of being a Christian.[107] Such

people, and many others, will be present in a congregation and the preacher must aim to make his sermon appropriate to their needs.

Deogratias, a deacon at Carthage, 'being judged to possess a rich power of catechizing',[108] was given heavy responsibility in this area of the Church's ministry. He found on some occasions his responsibilities to be wearisome and sought Augustine's advice. Augustine gave Deogratias encouragement by saying 'I too am almost always displeased with my discourse'[109] but insists that what is important is not our own judgement of our speech, but how it is received by its hearers. He went on to describe certain non-verbal forms of communication that derive from the speaker. Speech is a limited form of communication because of the difference between the conception of an idea in the mind and its expression in speech. The 'conception, as by a rapid flash, spreads itself over the mind, but speech on the other hand is slow and whilst it is being put forth, the conception has by this time hidden itself in its secret recesses'.[110] There are other ways of communication. 'Anger has one word to express it in Latin and another in Greek. . . . But the look of the angry man is not Latin or Greek . . . if the feeling of the mind becoming enraged go forth into the face, and produce a certain look, then all who see the angry man understand.'[111] An audience will respond more to the spirit of a speaker than his words. 'We are listened to with much greater pleasure, when we are at the same delighted with our occupation; for the thread of our discourse is affected by the very joy which we feel, and goes forth more easily and more acceptably.'[112] It is the man who is moved himself by the love of God for him who has the power to move others. People 'are the more enkindled, when . . . they see those minds also which they are aiming to affect, moved by the same fire'.[113] The point is expressed in the epigram that may be a paraphrase of this passage : 'One loving heart sets another on fire'. The love of God inspiring a speaker will kindle love in his audience or bring judgement upon one who is seeking to be a Christian for less than love's sake.[114]

Not always is a Christian minister eager to carry his responsibilities, whether they be those of preaching, teaching or anything else. 'Sometimes . . . we are called away from some other business which we wish to proceed with.'[115] This was surely a heart-felt statement for Augustine, but he insisted that 'we ought not to disclose to (those who are looking to us for ministry) . . . our feelings'.[116] It may be that this responsibility of the Christian minister to be available at all times was impressed upon him by his experience with Ambrose. Prior to his conversion, Augustine wanted to speak with Ambrose about his difficulties, only to find the Bishop absorbed in his study. 'Often when we came to his room—for no one was forbidden to enter, nor was it his custom that the arrival of visitors should be announced to him—we would see him thus reading to himself. After we had sat for a long time in silence—for who would dare interrupt one so intent?—we would then depart, realising that he was unwilling to be distracted.'[117] If the catechist, or preacher, found himself chafing at his responsibilities he 'must seek in accordance with God's will for remedies, such as may make to expand the heart which is shrunk up'.[118] Chief among these is the example of Christ taking the form of a servant, but one may also consider the simple absorbing devotion of a mother for her child or the hen for her chicks.[119]

There are other problems that limit the effectiveness of a speaker. He can be overconcerned to be correct in his forms of expression. The important thing is not to let 'our mind err from the truth in the things themselves'.[120] Less important is whether there was 'anything imperfect or incorrect in sounds which had utterance given them'.[121] If the speaker makes a mistake and it is pointed out he must 'receive correction with gentleness of mind'.[122] If it is unnoticed he must simply avoid the error in future. Better it is to speak freely than be restrained by an obsession for correctness. The speaker may also find himself having to repeat things that have become commonplace to him.[123] It is here that a developed affinity between preacher and congregation will stand him in good stead. If our hearers are our friends, and what is commonplace to us is not to them, we shall be caught up by their delight in the new thing they are learning. 'Is it not constantly the case, that, when we are showing to persons who have never seen them, certain large and beautiful prospects either of cities or fields, which we from often seeing them had come to pass by without pleasure, our own delight is renewed in the delight which novelty causes to them.'[124] The preacher must be looking out for signs that indicate whether or not he is convincing his hearers. It may be that the audience will have an unhealthy reverence for the speaker and will choose an attitude of passive resignation rather than indicate disagreement. We must attempt to remove this attitude 'by kind and cheering words, and suggest our common brotherhood so as to temper his reverence for us, and inspire him with confidence to utter freely any objection which he has to make'.[125] This is easier to do in a catechetical situation than when preaching, but we have seen that Augustine did establish such a relationship with his congregation that feed-back of this sort was possible. The preacher will look out for signs of weariness in his congregation and respond 'by saying something seasoned with discreet cheerfulness, and suited to the matter in hand, or something very wonderful and amusing, or, it may be, something painful and mournful : and such as may affect himself rather than another, in order that being pinched by concern for self he may continue watchful.'[126] Augustine here introduced the radical suggestion for the North African Church that seats might be provided for the congregation to relieve weariness, as in 'certain Churches beyond the sea'.

On preaching

Beside directing his attention to the needs of hearers and speaker Augustine in *De catechizandis rudibus* described the content of instruction to converts and gives us, like Luther, a *Greater* and *Short* catechism. The way in which the sermon itself should be presented is given in *De doctrina Christiana Book IV*, and this we must now consider.

It is in this book that we find the beginnings of the rhetoric of the sermon or 'homiletics' seen as a distinct branch of study. The classical rhetoricians had considered rhetoric to be the art of persuasive speech.[127] Augustine retained this concept, but broadened it to include, beside persuasion, instruction and exposition. In doing this homiletics was born and Augustine's seminal contribution was to incorporate the best of the classical rhetorical tradition into the art of the sermon. Augustine rejected the 'sophist' rhetorical tradition with its preoccupation with style

and other elements of display. In the fourth and fifth centuries
BC Isocrates had refined the rather artificial style of Gorgias
into an elegant vehicle for speech. His followers emphasized this
element of eloquence, whereas Cicero and Quintillian gave
prominence to the theme Plato had used to attack the sophists:
the purpose of rhetoric is to move men to truth.[128] Augustine did
not attack sophistry. He defined it as a discourse 'which is more
abundant than is consistent with gravity, being inflated with
verbal ornament'[129] and then proceeded to expound his views
of a proper rhetoric, that lay within the Ciceronian tradition.[130]

Augustine saw his task in *De Doctrina Christiana IV* as that
of describing a way of teaching the things that had been learned
in the Scriptures.[131] He first corrected the expectations of his
readers by saying that he was not going to provide rules of
rhetoric. It was not that he rejected their utility. 'Since by means
of the art of rhetoric both truth and falsehood are urged, who
would dare to say that truth should stand in the person of its
defenders unarmed against lying, so that they who wish to urge
falsehoods may know how to make their listeners benevolent, or
attentive, or docile in their presentation, while the defenders of
truth are ignorant of the art?'[132] What Augustine saw was the
danger of learning rules in a manual of rhetoric so that technical
mastery of the rules came to be regarded as more important than
truth. Here one can see another example of Augustine's *uti/frui*
distinction. Rhetoric is to be used not enjoyed.[133] A young man
might spend time studying the rhetoricians, but 'we do not hold
them to be of such importance that we would wish mature and
grave men to spend their time learning them'.[134] The better
method of learning eloquence is by the imitation of the eloquent.[135] In this way eloquence would grow up from within,
rather than be imposed on a speech from without. 'I think that
there is hardly a single eloquent man who can both speak well
and think of the rules of eloquence while he is speaking.'[136] 'Boys
do not need the art of grammar which teaches correct speech
if they have the opportunity to grow up and live among men
who speak correctly.'[137] The preacher should make use of eloquence, but he ought not to value it incorrectly. Augustine called
Cicero to support him: 'Eloquence without wisdom is often
extremely injurious and profits no one.'[138] He summed up his

view in a typically elegant way: 'He who speaks eloquently is heard with pleasure; he who speaks wisely is heard with profit.'[139]

Where can we find examples of eloquence to be imitated? Augustine answered that they are to be found in the Bible, where the writers were not only wise but eloquent. He examined Romans 5:3–5 and 1 Corinthians 11:16–17 to show that they have a prose rhythm that can be described under the heads of classical sentence movement. Having done this Augustine admitted that it would be tedious to show the same things in other passages[140] and then proceeded to do this with Amos 6:1–11!

The conclusion Augustine drew from this study of biblical writers was that, though they were eloquent, it was not for eloquence's sake, but 'that others might understand the mysteries of the faith'.[141] This must guide Christian preachers. 'In all their utterances they should first of all seek to speak so that they may be understood, speaking in so far as they are able with such clarity that either he who does not understand is very slow or that the difficulty and subtlety lie not in the manner of speaking but in the things which we wish to explain and show, so that this is the reason why we are understood less, or more slowly.'[142] In the service of clarity the preacher will choose his words carefully. 'The desire of a person seeking such clarity sometimes neglects a more cultivated language, not caring for what sounds elegant but for what well indicates and suggests what he wishes to show.'[143] 'He who teaches should thus avoid all words which do not teach. And if he can find other correct words which are understood he should select these; but if he cannot find them, either because they do not occur to him or because they do not exist, he should use words less correct, provided that the thing being taught is taught and learned without distortion when they are used.'[144] This struggle for clarity is particularly important in preaching because there is not the opportunity for the hearers to ask questions. 'However an attentive crowd eager to comprehend usually shows by its motion whether it understands, and until it signifies comprehension the matter being discussed should be considered and expressed in a variety of ways.'[145] This leads Augustine to point out the difficulty of the preacher who is speaking from a prepared script that he has memorized. He cannot be responsive to the congregation in such a way as to fulfil the purpose of preaching. 'Of what use is a gold key if it will not open what we wish?'[146]

To teach, please and persuade

From IV xii 27 Augustine moved on to the art of persuasion and refashioned the teaching of Cicero for the Christian preacher. He began by alluding to Cicero: 'a certain eloquent man, said and said truly, that he who is eloquent should speak in such a way that he teaches, delights and moves.'[147] Augustine then gave a direct quotation from Cicero's *Orator*: 'To teach is a necessity, to please is a sweetness, to persuade is a victory.'[148] Augustine made an odd distinction by separating delighting and moving from teaching as being those aspects of a speech that depend upon the manner in which we speak. He had already indicated the importance of clarity and was later to link a subdued style with teaching. He does seem to believe that teaching, if it is to be effective, depends upon the manner of its presentation. He was right, however, to emphasize that a speaker who desires 'to delight or to move the person to whom he speaks ... will not do it simply by speaking in any way at all; but the manner in which he speaks determines whether he does so'.[149]

Augustine's concern that rhetoric should be used in the service of truth made him insist that teaching should come before persuasion. When the truth is made clear the hearers may be so moved by the truth 'that it is not necessary to move them further by greater powers of eloquence'.[150] It is not to be assumed though that truth has always the power to move a man. Men may not act in accordance with what they know. 'People may be taught and pleased and still not consent.'[151] Also there are people who are 'not pleased by truth if it is stated in any way except in that way in which the words are also pleasing. Delight has no small place in eloquence'.[152] Here again the Christian preacher must press for some further response. 'The eloquence of the discourse pleases in vain unless that which is learned is implemented in action. It is necessary therefore for the ecclesiastical orator, when he urges that something be done, not only to teach that he may instruct and to please that he may hold attention, but also to persuade that he may be victorious.'[153] Augustine rounded on all those who spoke of trivial matters and seemed to aim at

nothing more than pleasing their hearers—where 'trivial and
fragile truths are ornamented with a frothy nexus of words'.[154]
Even his beloved Cyprian did not escape castigation on this count.[155]

Augustine brought together Cicero's three functions of speaking and his teaching about appropriate styles.[156] What Cicero
had learned about oratory in the courts Augustine applied to
the Christian preacher who has great things of which to speak.
He summarized what he had learned from Cicero in saying:
'Although our teacher should speak of great things, he should
not always speak about them in the grand manner, but in a
subdued manner when he teaches something, in a moderate
manner when he condemns or praises something. But when
something is to be done and he is speaking to those who ought
to do it but do not wish to do it, then those great things should
be spoken in the grand manner in a way appropriate to the
persuasion of their minds.'[157] Examples of subdued and moderate
styles are quoted from St Paul where his aim is, respectively,
to teach and win his readers. When St Paul wishes to teach he
employs a simple, explanatory tone, taking up questions and
dealing with them as they occur. When he is exhorting his
readers to accept for themselves the truth of which he is speaking,
St Paul adopts a more moderate style: e.g. 'Bless them that
persecute you; bless and curse not. Rejoice with them that
rejoice; weep with them that weep. Being of one mind one
towards another.'[158] When the speaker wants to move his hearers
so that they are persuaded to become different or act differently,
he must use a grand style which 'differs from the moderate style
not so much in that it is adorned with verbal ornaments but in
that it is forceful with emotions of the spirit. Although it uses
almost all of the ornaments, it does not seek them if it does not
need them. It is carried along by its own impetus, and if the
beauties of eloquence occur they are caught up by the force of
the things discussed and not deliberately assumed for decoration.
It is enough for the matter being discussed that the appropriate-
ness of the words be determined by the ardour of the heart rather
than by careful choice.'[159] Such a grand style Augustine saw St
Paul adopting in 2 Corinthians 6:2–11, Romans 8:28–39 and
Galatians 4:10–20. He gave further examples of the three styles
in Cyprian and Ambrose.[160]

Augustine did not envisage the preacher undertaking the three functions of preaching, and using the appropriate styles, in a temporal sequence. 'Speech should be varied with all types of style in so far as this may be done appropriately.'[161] This mixture of styles is required to maintain the interest of the hearer—although he pointed out that the subdued style can be sustained for longer periods than the grand style without losing interest.[162] By varying style 'the impetus of our speech ebbs and flows like the sea'.[163] In order to secure this the preacher may 'say some things in the subdued style which might be spoken in the grand style so that those things which are spoken in the grand style may seem more grand by comparison and be rendered more luminous as if by shadows'.[164]

Sensing that his readers may have become over-fascinated by stylistic consideration Augustine returned to his emphasis on the objectives of the preacher. Technique must always be the hand-maid of the gospel. The applause of the congregation should not make the preacher believe that his objective has been reached. He told of his experience in 'dissuading the populace of Caesarea in Mauretania from civil war' :[165] 'I did not think that I had done anything when I heard them applauding, but when I saw them weeping. They indicated by their applause that they were being taught and pleased, but tears indicated that they were persuaded.'[166]

'The end of eloquence is to persuade. . . . In any of these three styles an eloquent man speaks in a manner suitable to persuasion, but if he does not persuade, he has not attained the end of eloquence. Thus in the subdued style he persuades his listener that what he says is true; he persuades in the grand style that these things which we know should be done are done.'[167]

Important as Augustine saw it to help the preacher become more effective by knowledge of the rhetorical arts, he knew that there were some who would never be eloquent. He did not want these to be discouraged or the eloquent to believe that they possessed all that was necessary for a preacher. The quality of life of the preacher had greater weight than his eloquence.[168] In this he was standing in line with Cicero and Quintillian,[169] but above all with Aristotle and his emphasis on 'ethos' : 'The orator persuades by moral character when his speech is delivered in such a

manner as to render him worthy of confidence . . . moral character . . . constitutes the most effective means of proof.'[170] This
point is well expressed by Emerson: 'The reason why anyone
refuses his assent to your opinion, or his aid to your benevolent
design, is in you. He refuses to accept you as a bringer of truth,
because though you think you have it, he feels that you have it
not. You have not given him the authentic sign.'[171] Truth must
become incarnate to have the power to persuade. The preacher
must be himself possessed by the truth and live by it.[172] Thus
Christ living within the preacher takes his voice and speaks
through it. Without this living experience of Christ within, the
preacher's words do not possess the power of Christ to renew
the lives of his hearers.

This point, where Augustine leaves us in *De doctrina
Christiana*, leads to the final point we wish to make. When
Christian preaching, as Augustine understood it, takes place,
God himself is present in it. When God's word 'is preached and
inasmuch as the preacher speaks the truth, Christ speaks through
him'.[173] Preaching has this power to work within men because
the words become signs that, as it were, trigger off the truth that
is latent within man, taught 'by him who dwells within and gives
me counsel about words spoken externally in the ear'.[174] I believe
Polman overstates his case in maintaining that in the writings
of Augustine the Neoplatonic epistemology of *De magistro*
'largely gave way to Biblical concepts of God's Word',[175] particularly in the homilies on St John's Gospel. But the point that he
is making, that in preaching God is active, would command the
fervent approval of Augustine.

NOTES

1 e.g. Augustine's commentaries on Genesis were written as he
  was working out 'the problem of matter and form which is
  central to his metaphysic' (E. TeSelle, *Augustine the Theologian* (London, 1970) 135).

2 Some dispute exists over whether all the sermons on 1 John
  were preached by Augustine or prepared to be read to his
  people; cf. Altaner, op. cit., 512. Van Der Meer raises the same
  possibility concerning certain sermons on the Gospel of St
  John (op. cit., 512).

3 cf. Altaner, op. cit., 513

4 A critical edition of the sermons is appearing in *Corpus Christianorum* by C. Lambot (1961f.). In translation we have the sermons on Psalms 1–37 in *Ancient Christian Writers*; the whole Psalter in the *Library of the Fathers*; *Nine Sermons of St Augustine on the Psalms* translated by E. Hill (London, 1958); on the Gospel of John we have the two volumes in the Dods edition of Augustine's works and a selection in *John shines through Augustine* translated by A. P. Carleton (London, 1960); the sermons on 1 John appear in the *Library of Christian Classics* 8 (London, 1955); for the individual sermons, apart from 'Sermons for Christmas and the Epiphany' in *Ancient Christian Writers*, we depend upon 'Sermons on Selected Lessons of the New Testament' in the *Library of the Fathers* and sermons 184–265 in *The Fathers of the Church* (New York, 1959).

5 cf. H. Pope, *St Augustine of Hippo* (New York, 1961) 135

6 ibid.

7 En. in Ps. 88; 240 and 256

8 M. Pellegrino, *The True Priest* (Langley, 1968) 43

9 Vita 7; 202

10 notarii, the Roman equivalent of shorthand-typists; Ep. 139.3; II 216

11 Ep. 158.1; II 263

12 Ep. 41.2; I 137

13 Ep. 169.13; II 343/4

14 cf. Morin's frustration with inaccuracy of transcription, quoted Pope, op. cit., 133 and the identical text of two independent Mss. on Serm. 37—cf. G. Bonner, *St Augustine of Hippo* (London, 1960) 145.

15 Vita 31; 244

16 E. B. Pusey, in his introduction to LF Sermons I iii

17 Van Der Meer, op. cit., 412

18 Serm. (Frang. 2.4) quoted by Brown, op. cit. (Augustine), 256; cf. Augustine's complaint that visiting bishops would not give him 'a helping hand' by preaching—cf. E. Hill in *Blackfriars*, November 1954, 464.

19 En. in Ps. 138.1; VI 191

20 Tr. in Jo. Ev. IX 9; I 133

21 Serm. 95.1; I 365

22 Tr. in Jo. Ev. III 13; I 285

23 op. cit., 264

24 En. in Ps. 99.1; IV 463

25 Serm. 126.8; II 546; cf. the images of bread, light, water, rain, clouds that Augustine used in describing preaching and the preacher as a physician—cf. the idea of redemption by Christ, *medicus humilis* (Arbesmann, op. cit.)—sower, husbandman, builder (Pellegrino, op. cit., 92f.).

26 C.D. II 28; 85

27 Serm. 17.2; quoted Van Der Meer, op. cit., 420/1

28 I remember how odd it seemed and how reminiscent of the ethos of the Patristic age, when, lecturing at an Oxford Patristic Conference, G. Florovsky suddenly turned towards J. Daniélou in the audience and conducted a personal one-sided dispute with him.

29 En. in Ps. 61.23; III 210/1

30 Brown, op. cit. (Augustine), 292

31 En. in Ps. 136.9; VI 166

32 Brown, op. cit. (Augustine), 313

33 Ep. 21.3; I 48

34 Ep. 21.5; I 49

35 op. cit., 38

36 Serm. 114.1; I 472

37 Serm. 179.1; II 928

38 En. in Ps. 103 i 19; V 87

39 Serm. 151. 4; II 712

40 Serm. 179.7; II 933

41 En. in Ps. 50.13; II 378

42 Serm. 179. 2–3; II 929

43 Serm. (Frang. 6.2); quoted in Van Der Meer. op. cit., 430

44 1 Corinthians 4 : 7, e.g. Ad Simpl. I 2.9; 393

45 Serm. 133.1; II 725

46 Vita 31; 242

47 Serm. (Misc. Agost. I 542.13); quoted in Pellegrino, op. cit., 128

48 Serm. 111.1; II 709

49 cf. T. T. Rowe, op. cit. (St Augustine), 42

50 Rhetoric III 14; 427

51 ibid.

52 ibid.

53 Vita 15; 211/2

54 De doct. chr. IV xxx 63; 168

55 De doct. chr. IV xv 32; 140

56 Tr. in Jo. Ev. XIX 5; I 266

57 XIX 15; I 278

58 XIX 20; I 283

59 En. in Ps. 39.10; II 142

60 Serm. 131.5; II 588

61 En. in Ps. 88 i 10; IV 248

62 Serm. 84. 2; I 606

63 En. in Ps. 72.34; III 490

64 Serm. 311.4; quoted in Van Der Meer, op. cit., 429

65 Tr. in Jo. Ev. XLV 13; II 86

66 op. cit. (Augustine), 252

67 Serm. 151.8; II 716

68 Brown, op. cit. (Augustine), 251

69 Tr. in Jo. Ev. IV 16; I 54

70 Serm. 56. 11; I 74

71 En. in Ps. 36 iii 19; II 66

72 En. in Ps. 126. 13; VI 31

73 Serm. 101.4; I 405

74 cf. Brown, op. cit. (Augustine), 248

75 Serm. 66.5; I 149

76 Serm. 82.15; I 265/6

77 Serm. 125.8; II 535

78 cf. TeSelle, op. cit., 273f.

79 op. cit. (Augustine), 255

80 ibid.

81 En. in Ps. 18 ii 1; I 129

82 En. in Ps. 98.4; IV 448/9

83 Serm. 56.12; I 76

84 Serm. 180.13; II 947

85 Serm. (Guelfergitanus 19.2); quoted Pope, op. cit., 160/1

86 En. in Ps. 70 i 17; translated by E. Hill in Marrou, op. cit. (Influence) 123/4; also LF Psalms III 424/5

87 J. H. S. Burleigh in *Theology*, September 1952, 342

88 En. in Ps. 95.15; IV 411

89 Serm. 50.6; quoted in Van De Meer, op. cit., 424, with many other examples.

90 Serm. 178.8; II 925

91 En. in Ps. 83.3; IV 148

92 C. ep. q. v. Fun. ii 2; 130

93 En. in Ps. 36 iii 6; II 53

94 17; 208

95 En. in Ps. 88 i 29; IV 255/6

96 Serm. 161.10; II 808

97 cf. P. Kelvin, *The Bases of Social Behaviour* (London, n.d.) 61

98 En. in Ps. 103 i 13; V 81
99 cf. Brown, op. cit. (Augustine), 253
100 cf. Augustine's exposition of certain biblical numbers in En. in Ps. 49.9f; II 342f.
101 De cat. rud. xv 23; 214
102 cf. J. Parry, *The Psychology of Human Communication* (London, 1967) 84f.
103 Aristotle, *Rhetoric* I 3; 33
104 De cat. rud. xv 23; 215
105 vii 12; 199
107 xvi 24; 215
108 De cat. rud. i. 1; 187
109 De cat. rud. ii 3; 188
110 De cat. rud. ii 3; 189
112 De cat. rud. ii 4; 190
113 De cat. rud. ii 7; 193
114 cf. De cat. rud. v 9; 195/6
115 De cat. rud. x 14; 204
116 ibid.
117 Conf. VI iii 3; 116
118 De cat. rud. x 14; 204
119 De cat. rud. x 15; 205
120 De cat. rud. xi 16; 206
121 ibid.
122 ibid.
123 De cat. rud. xii 17; 208
124 ibid.
125 De cat. rud. xiii 18; 209
126 De cat. rud. xiii 19; 209
127 cf. E. P. J. Corbett, *Classical Rhetoric for the Modern Student* (New York, 1965) 21
128 cf. Corbett, op. cit., 536f.
129 De doct. chr. II xxxi 48; 67
130 cf. C. S. Baldwin in *The Province of Rhetoric*, ed. J. Schwartz and J. A. Rycenga (New York, 1965) 158; L. Thonssen and A. C. Baird, *Speech Criticism* (New York, 1948) 110
131 De doct. chr. IV 1; 117
132 De doct. chr. IV ii 3; 118
133 cf. G. Howie, *Educational Theory and Practice in St Augustine* (London, 1969) 231
134 De doct. chr. IV iii 4; 119
135 ibid.

136 ibid.; 120
137 De doct. chr. IV iii 5; 120
138 De doct. chr. IV v 7; 121
139 De doct. chr. IV v 8; 122
140 De doct. chr. IV vii 14; 128
141 De doct. chr. IV viii 22; 132/3
142 ibid.
143 De doct. chr. IV x 24; 133
144 ibid.
145 De doct. chr. IV x 25; 134/5
146 De doct. chr. IV xi 26; 136
147 De doct. chr. IV xii 27; 136
148 ibid.
149 ibid.
150 De doct. chr. IV xii 28; 137
151 ibid.
152 De doct. chr. IV xiii 29; 137/8
153 ibid.
154 De doct. chr. IV xiv 31; 139
155 ibid.
156 De doct. chr. IV xvii 34; 143
157 De doct. chr. IV xix 38; 145
158 De doct. chr. IV xx 40; 148
159 De doct. chr. IV xx 42; 150
160 De doct. chr. IV xxi 45f.; 152f.
161 De doct. chr. IV xxii 51; 158
162 ibid.
163 ibid.
164 De doct. chr. IV xxiii 52; 159
165 De doct. chr. IV xxiv 53; 160
166 ibid.
167 De doct. chr. IV xxv 55; 161/2
168 De doct. chr. IV xxvii 59; 164
169 cf. Howie, op. cit., 233
170 Aristotle, *Rhetoric* I ii 4; 17
171 quoted L. L. Lacour in *Pastoral Psychology*, October 1965, 17
172 cf. De doct. chr. IV xxix 62; 168
173 Serm. 17.1; quoted A. D. R. Polman, *The Word of God according to St Augustine* (London, 1961) 127, with many other references.
174 De mag. 46; 101
175 op. cit., 156

CHAPTER THREE

On Sacraments

STANDING in the room of the *colloquy* in the Schloss at Marburg one can feel that, though the debate about the eucharist between Luther and Zwingli was in one sense an ecclesiastical domestic affair, it was also a point of transition in the human story. This plain room was the setting for a significant stage in the process of secularization. At one level we can see theologians comparing the values of certain notions about the eucharist: realism (Luther), signification (Zwingli), figuration (Oecolampadius).[1] But the heat of the controversy must have had a different source. In Luther's mind, Zwingli's reductionism would lead to a loss of 'that unity of word and deed, of picture and thing, of the bread and the glorified body ... body will become merely body, and symbol merely symbol'.[2] The issue was whether Christianity could afford a loss of mystery and settle for definitions that isolated units of truth from their complex relationships with others.

It is all too easy to resort to a process of mystification when theological expression gets difficult—it can be the equivalent of the alleged marginal note in the sermon manuscript: 'argument weak—shout!' On the other hand there is the danger of refusing to speak except in stating the obvious. But theology works on the frontier of what can properly be called *mystery*. The attitudes I adopt prevent me from appreciating certain experiences, just as 'a certain subjective state is the necessary condition for making certain values visible at all'.[3] Christian affirmations are concerned with the meaning of embodied events. In Christian thought 'mystery is simultaneously the human sign and the divine reality which it reveals and bestows'[4] and the attitude necessary for penetrating the mystery is faith, without which it is opaque.

It is in sacraments that this characteristic of Christian statements is most clearly seen. We are presented at the same time with the sign and the reality it signifies, if faith enables us to be receptive. The whole sacramental event was spoken of in the

early church as a mystery through which the mysterious reality
of God was revealed. In the pagan mysteries 'the destinies and
acts of their god' were actualized in sacred actions. So in
Christian sacraments the redeeming acts of God in Christ were
cultically repeated so that the man of faith was taken up into
the event of redemption.[5]

Symbolism and realism

Up to the fourth century Christian writers preserved an understanding of the sacraments as mysteries by avoiding being too
precise. Symbolism and realism lay side by side in both Tertullian and Cyprian.[6] For Tertullian, Christ gave 'bread the
figure of his body'[7] and yet the bread could be spoken of directly
as 'the Lord's body'.[8] It is this holding together of the two
elements that preserves the sacraments as *mysteries*. With
Ambrose a current of thinking appeared in the Western Church
that broke this tension, with far-reaching effects up to the present
day. In his two treatises (*De Sacramentis* and *De Mysteriis*) he
speaks of the conversion of the elements into the body and blood
of Christ and emphasizes that the words of institution effect this
consecration or change.[9] Both these features are to be found in
certain Greek Fathers. Cyril of Jerusalem expressed it: 'We call
upon the merciful God to send forth his Holy Spirit upon the
gifts laying before him; that he may make the bread the body
of Christ, and the wine the blood of Christ; for whatsoever the
Holy Ghost has touched, is sanctified and changed.'[10] Gregory
of Nyssa similarly speaks of 'the bread which is sanctified by the
Word of God (being) transmuted into the body of God the
Word'.[11] Though Ambrose reflected this realistic view of the
eucharist very strongly, he attempted to retain an element of
mystery by emphasizing the spiritual character of the food:
'Christ is in that sacrament, because it is the body of Christ;
therefore it is not bodily food, but spiritual. Whence also the
Apostle says of the type of it that "Our fathers ate spiritual meat,
and drank spiritual drink".'[12] It is clear that once language like
that of Ambrose was made current it would be taken more and
more literally. Just as in the Gospels people preferred 'wonders'
to 'signs', so a doctrine of the eucharist that simplified the elusive
concept of *mystery* would become attractive. 'The sacrament

which you receive is consecrated by the word of Christ. But if the word of Elijah was powerful enough to bring down fire from heaven, will not the word of Christ be powerful enough to change the characters of the elements . . . The Lord Jesus himself cries "This is my body". Before the blessing of the heavenly words another kind of thing is named, after consecration it is designated "body". He himself speaks of his blood. Before consecration it is spoken of as something else, after consecration it is named "blood". And you say "Amen", that is, it is true. What the mouth speaks let the mind within confess.'[13] Thus the way is open for the basic characteristic of Christian statements— mystery penetrated by faith—to be avoided and replaced by a view of the sacraments in which propositional beliefs are coded in liturgical action.

Augustine on signs

Though Augustine owed much to Ambrose for opening up the possibility of non-literal interpretation of scripture, it was not likely that he would follow him in this line of eucharistic thought. Ambrose had a somewhat prosaic mind. He tended to take up ideas and use them in a pragmatic way, without much consideration for their harmony with each other.[14] A typological approach to the Bible in general was acceptable to Ambrose, but a literal response to the institution of the eucharist was not seen as inconsistent. Though Augustine was not a rigidly systematic thinker, there was a basic consistency in his thinking. The subtle mind that could tease significance out of the most unlikely scriptural texts was not likely to approach the sacraments in a matter-of-fact way. At an early stage in searching for an adequate epistemology, he developed a doctrine of 'signs' that provided a mental framework that was able to lead him to an appreciation of the concept of *mystery* that was characteristic of earlier patristic thinking. The first discussion of the nature of 'signs' appears in an early work : *De magistro*. This was at a time when philosophical questions had a lively interest for Augustine. But it is unlikely, being the sort of man he was, that he had not given some thought to his own baptism two years before and the eucharistic life of the Church he now enjoyed.

The concept of sign had been used from Aristotle onwards.

It appeared in early Christian literature as, for example, in a simple form in 1 Clement where Rahab's scarlet rope was taken as a sign to indicate something more than itself.[15] Origen spoke of miracles as signs because they directed the mind to their author and his meaning in bringing them about.[16] But Markus records: 'Before Augustine, I have found only one hint of an attempt to bring the notion of "signification" to a central place in a theory of language.'[17] This hint is in Plotinus: 'The word is principally an impulse launched on the air, but it is not simply impulse; because it is articulated it somehow fashions the air; consequently it is a deed, but a significant one.'[18]

For Augustine words are one form of the sign. When a teacher instructs he uses signs of various kinds to convey knowledge—words, gestures, actions; but, in fact, nothing is learned from signs. 'If I am given a sign and I do not know the thing of which it is a sign, it can teach me nothing.'[19] The words or signs, which are external, have prompted the man to discover the truth that inwardly God has taught him.[20] In *Retractions* Augustine summarized his purpose in writing *De magistro*: to show 'that there is no teacher who teaches knowledge except God'.[21] At the end of that work he promised to discuss at another time 'the usefulness of words'.[22] This promise was fulfilled in *De doctrina Christiana*. There he defines a sign: 'A sign is a thing which causes us to think of something beyond the impression the thing itself makes upon the senses.'[23] There are natural signs which 'without any desire or intention of signifying, make us aware of something beyond themselves, like smoke which signifies fire'.[24] There are also conventional signs by which 'living creatures show to one another for the purpose of conveying, in so far as they are able, the motion of their spirits or something which they have sensed or understood'.[25] These latter Dr Markus calls 'diaphanous': one sees through them what is signified.[26] Words are signs of this kind. Holy Scripture is seen as a sign: the Word of God. But chiefly the Word of God is Christ, who is *the* sign. As 'our own word is made as it were a bodily utterance, through assuming that utterance as a means of displaying itself to men's senses' so 'the Word of God was made flesh, through assuming that flesh as a means of displaying himself to men's senses'.[27] The Word made flesh is there for all to see—an external thing—but the truth contained in this sign must be revealed, like all truth, to the 'inward eye' by God the Teacher. This readiness to be taught—the attitude necessary for perception—is faith.

Signs and sacraments

In Augustine the concept of the sign holds together his epistemology, understanding of Scripture and Christology. It is odd that, though the concept was applied also to his teaching about sacraments, it was not used in his ecclesiology.[28] We do not have the sequence found in E. Schillebeeckx[29] where sacramental theology is derived from ecclesiology which, in its turn, is an extension of Christology. In many places Augustine makes the link between the idea of sign and the sacraments. For example: God 'has bound his people under the new dispensation together in fellowship by sacraments, which are in number very few, in observance most easy, and in significance most excellent'.[30] Augustine always sees 'the sacraments as a species of signs'.[31]

But sacraments have a special quality that makes them very important in Augustine's scheme of understanding. They involve physical elements, but the mind is carried by them into an immaterial world. 'Through their material component they meet bodily man in his own condition, not, however, to let him remain there, but to draw him through their spiritual component towards the higher world.'[32] So instead of the creaturely world directing man away from the proper object of his love, in the sacraments creatures are used to draw man towards God. Similarly, the sacraments enacted in time provide a transition for the contemplation of eternal values. In this way Augustine's sacramental theology coheres with the Neoplatonic framework with which he works.

Augustine used the word sacrament of many things. On the basis of the background that has been described one would expect certain uses of words to be regarded as sacraments. So, for example, he sees in the titles of the Psalms a decking of 'the brow of a Psalm with the high announcement of a sacrament'.[33] The whole world of symbols used in proclamation belongs to the realms of sacraments: 'Whensoever illustrative symbols are borrowed, for the declaration of spiritual mysteries from created things ... this is done to give to the doctrine of salvation an eloquence adapted to raise the affections of those who receive it from things seen, corporal and temporal, to things unseen, spiritual and eternal.'[34] The sanctification of time in Christian festivals has sacramental character. God 'has bound his people ... together in fellowship by sacraments ... the annual commemoration, by special solemnities, of the Lord's passion, resurrection, and ascension, and of the descent of the Holy Spirit from heaven, and whatever else is in like manner observed by the whole Church wherever it has been established'.[35] So the whole cultic life of the Church was seen in a sacramental framework.[36] Within this framework certain institutions are of supreme importance, like baptism and the eucharist, and these are interpreted on the basis of sign/sacrament/mystery. The sacraments of the Old Testament have been replaced by others 'greater in efficacy, more beneficial in their use, easier in performance, and fewer in number' and the Christian should be ready 'to suffer all things for Christ's baptism, for Christ's eucharist, for Christ's sacred sign, since these are proofs of the accomplishment of what the former sacraments only pointed forward to in the future'.[37] To attempt, as Portalié does, to show that Peter Lombard's seven sacraments are found in Augustine is misguided. If the Church in the twelfth century had a common practice of regarding seven actions as sacramental, Augustine would not have seen any necessity for justifying the practice from ancient authorities. The Church's living tradition creates its sacramental structure.[39] But whatever the penumbra of sacramental references might be, baptism and the eucharist lay unchallenged within the umbra of Augustine's thought.

BAPTISM

Controversy with the Donatists and Pelagians stretched over the major part of Augustine's episcopate and the point about which so much gathered was the question of baptism. The theology of baptism that emerged gained from the great attention Augustine had to give to this subject over many years and the sharpness of the attacks he was forced to meet; but it was also limited by the polemical atmosphere in which he did his thinking. He was compelled by the controversies to produce a more rigid and self-contained doctrine than was usual for him. He needed to relate what he had to say about baptism to the nature of the Church and the nature of grace. It is easy for those who enquire about his teaching concerning baptism not to be able to see the wood for the trees.

In the *City of God* Augustine saw all human history in terms of the interaction of two solidarities. 'The two cities were created by two kinds of love: the earthly city was created by self-love reaching to the point of contempt of God, the Heavenly City by the love of God carried as far as contempt of self.'[40] Baptism can be seen as that action which sets out in one moment of time the division in mankind that runs through the whole of history. At one level it can be seen as an administrative action by which 'the faithful' are defined. The faithful 'to whom we distribute the Body of Christ'[41] are defined by baptism. 'They who are baptised are, by virtue of the excellence and administration of so great a sacrament . . . reckoned in the number of the faithful.'[42] By baptism people become part of the eucharistic community.[43] It signifies the purpose of God being worked out in history, by which man is reformed in the image of God—not simply as an individual but also as a person living in community. All the elements within Augustine's teaching on baptism can be seen as held together by this concept. The weakness of this thesis, that there is a correspondence between City of God/earthly city and baptised/unbaptised, is that it tends to identify the City of God and the institutional church. Although Augustine did not make this identity he saw it as the closest approximation, in visible terms, that was possible, and so the thesis can be accepted as long as its limitations are understood.

Initiation
Whatever other levels of meaning baptism possessed, at the time of Augustine, it was seen very clearly as an initiatory rite. The Christian community still preserved elements of the secrecy required during the centuries of persecution. Baptism was seen as the visible door leading into a temple of secrets.[44] The mystery of the eucharist was reserved only for the baptised and only as part of their preparation for baptism did the catechumens learn the Creed and the Lord's Prayer.[45] In a vivid image Augustine

described the process of initiation. 'Remember, you did not exist, and you were created : you were carried to the Lord's threshing floor . . . when you were set aside as catechumens you were stored in his barn. You gave in your names : you began to be ground with fasting and exorcism. After that you came to water, were moistened and made one. You were cooked then, when the ardour of the Holy Spirit came near, and now have been made the Lord's bread.'[46] In this process it was baptism that was decisive. As the Hebrews were delivered and became the People of God in passing through the Red Sea, so in baptism 'the faithful pass into a new life'.[47] Through baptism Christ 'presents to himself a glorious church'.[48] By making baptism the culmination of an annual programme of preparation, coming to its climax on Easter Eve, the element of initiation into the life of the Church was given dramatic form. It was abundantly clear that those who were baptised were entering a society that was on pilgrimage. The divestment before baptism and the exorcisms served to emphasise that the baptismal candidate was changing his allegiance—he was joining those who were different from other men in that they were seeking the City of God.[49]

Character

For Augustine baptism imprinted a mark, a character, on the baptised signifying that he was the property of Christ. In the famous letter to Boniface Augustine implies that in baptism one receives 'the mark of the Redeemer' or 'the royal stamp'.[50] The 'mark of the Lord' is impressed on the baptised whoever administers it.[51] Baptism replaces circumcision, but circumcision is a prefiguring of baptism and, as this cannot be repeated but remains the irremovable mark of belonging to the old People of God, so baptism serves the same purpose—it is the sign of the bond by which the Christian is held by Christ.[52] Baptism is seen as 'the banner of (the) King',[53] just as a Roman army displayed the *vexillum* on its standard.[54] When confronted by the Donatist insistence on rebaptism Augustine was adamant that he could never contemplate such a practice, 'because I do not do despite to the stamp of the monarch'.[55] For the essence of his view is that in baptism it is Christ who baptises,[56] and it is his stamp that is placed on the baptised. Again we see baptism was an action in time that has the quality of a sign—through it we see the ongoing process of Christ gathering his Church.

Regeneration

The one human solidarity to which the Christian gospel responds, in Augustine's view, is that of sin. Even children, who because of 'a likeness of humility'[57] are commended by Christ, are yet 'made captive under the devil's power, until they are redeemed therefrom by the laver of regeneration'.[58] Augustine seems to have arrived at this view as the logical implication of the Church's practice of infant baptism. He begins with the assumption that the Church is not doing nothing when it baptises. What then is it that happens behind and within the external rite? The traditional teaching he had received was that baptism was for the remission of sin. 'Unable to contravene that authority of the universal Church, which has been unquestionably handed down by the Lord and his apostles' the conclusion must be 'that infants require the same benefits of the Mediator, in order that, being washed by the sacrament and charity of the faithful, and thereby incorporated into the body of Christ, which is the Church, they may be reconciled to God, and so live in him, and be saved, and delivered, and redeemed, and enlightened'.[59] So the sin that is not obvious in their conduct must be assumed in the form of original sin. 'Let the little ones come, let the sick come to the Physician, the lost to their Redeemer: let them come, let no man hinder them. In the branch they have not yet committed any evil, but they are ruined in their root.'[60] This hidden disease is healed by the grace of God which acts hiddenly within the sign of the sacramental action. The detailed working out of what Augustine meant by original sin and the way in which it is transmitted, can easily hide the structural basis of his theology of baptism. The 'poisoner wounded the whole mass of mankind in the first man; no one passes to the Second (man, Christ) from the first, but by the sacrament of baptism. In babes born, and not yet baptised, let Adam be acknowledged; in babes born and baptised, and thereby born again, let Christ be acknowledged'.[61] What was being represented and achieved in the non-baptised/baptised transition was the salvation achieved in the death and resurrection of Christ. Salvation comes 'by

placing man within the present reality of the death and resurrection of Christ, so that what once happened in Christ is repeated
in Christian man through the sacrament'.[62]

Augustine saw this hidden transition being achieved by Christ
whose presence was signified in the sacrament. It was to the
death and resurrection of Christ in the past that baptism referred.
But the signification was not merely a reference back—a memor-
ial of the baptism of Christ that had prefigured his death and
resurrection. Christ was the invisible reality signified by the
visible element of the sacrament. His presence was pointed to by
the three-fold name of God, in whom the candidate was baptised. 'The word is added to the element, and there results the
sacrament, as if itself also a kind of visible word.'[63] When the
Christian man regards baptism 'he knows what it refers to so
that he venerates it not in carnal servitude but in spiritual freedom'[64]—he does not see just the outward rite, but he is illuminated by the Spirit to see Christ's presence in it.[65] The faith given
to the baptised by the Holy Spirit enables the redemptive work
of Christ to take effect in him. In the case of a child, in whom
a personal act of faith cannot be evoked, the Church acts as a
mother and uses her heart and mouth 'that they may be imbued
with the sacred mysteries'.[66] Far from this being a smooth way of
getting round a difficulty in his argument the point is fundamental to it. The hands of the Church reaching out towards the
candidate for baptism express the search for the unity of all men
in Christ. The Holy Spirit is the creator of this unity, binding
the Church together and drawing men into its unity. When a
child is 'presented to receive the sacred rite, (it) is the work of
the Spirit by whom the child thus presented is regenerated. . . .
The regenerating Spirit is possessed in common by the parents
who present the child, and by the infant that is presented. . . .
We are made partakers of grace along with others through the
unity of the Holy Spirit.'[67] The one who, by his own faith or
that of parents or the Church, comes for baptism is incorporated
into the unity of the body of Christ. In this sacramental rite the
ultimate purpose of human community is actualized.[68] But not
only so, the unity created is with the Head of the Body—Christ
—and the dying and the rising of him take effect in the baptised.
'If we have been united with him in the likeness of his death,

we shall be also united with him in the likeness of his resurrection.'[69] The sign displays, not only cosmic redemption on the grand scale, it makes effective that redemption in a particular human being.

EUCHARIST

Augustine's thought about the eucharist, 'unsystematic and many-sided as it is, is tantalisingly difficult to assess'.[70] It has been all too easy to select or interpret texts to support a preconceived notion of what the eucharist is about. An obvious example of this is the interpretation of Augustine's eucharistic doctrine by E. Portalié,[71] where Augustine is used to support Catholic orthodoxy. But to recognize the problem is no safeguard against making the same error. We face the basic danger of all historical theology: labelling ideas and assuming that thereby we have understood them. It seems best to look for some of the most frequently recurring ideas and to allow them to speak. Augustine was capable of producing highly structured concepts. On the eucharist, as on baptism, he was governed by his fundamental conception of signs and attempted to evoke in his hearers or readers that to which the sign pointed, without limiting the signification by over-precision.

Incorporation in the Church

From the way in which Augustine, so often, links together and uses the same terms of baptism and the eucharist, we can expect to find theological connections. Among these is the place of both sacraments in incorporating the faithful within the Church. God 'has bound his people under the new dispensation together in fellowship by sacraments'.[72] Those in the communion of the Church 'drink what flowed from the side of Christ'.[73] The eucharist is not just an external rite performed by Christians—a characteristic practice of belonging. It signifies, and is creative of, the unity that binds men together in the Church. 'This bread signified to you how you ought to love unity. It was made out of many grains of wheat, which were originally separate, but were united by application of water . . . and baked with fire. . . . You are made bread, which is the Body of Christ: and here is the symbol of unity.'[74] This emphasis on the eucharist as the symbol of unity was increased by the problem of the Donatist schism, but its source is deep in Augustine's sacramental theology. The Christian needs to be bound in fellowship with the rest of the faithful, for in this way he becomes united with the Head of the Body and, as in baptism, receives his redemption by identification.

Realism

When Augustine speaks in realistic terms of the presence of Christ in the bread and wine of the eucharist there is a depth to his thought not found in Ambrose. He locates the presence of Christ in the eucharist in order to state that the whole Body is present in it—Head and members—and that the faithful come into contact with every element by which their redemption can be realized. Christ 'walked here in very flesh, and gave that very flesh to us to eat for our salvation; and no one eats that flesh, unless he has first worshipped'.[75] But Christ is present in the sign as a whole and not merely in the bread and wine as bread and wine. While the elements and that which they signify are inextricably bound to each other, Augustine guards against a materialistic approach that destroys the mystery, by distinguishing between the eucharistic elements and the effect they produce in the communicant. Receiving Christ 'belongs to the sacrament, not to the visible sacrament' and the man who receives life through it is 'he who eats within, not without; who eats in his heart, not who presses with his teeth'.[76] If the presence of Christ was localized in the elements, the role of faith in enabling the penetration of mystery would be eroded. Faith enables the virtue of the sacrament to take effect in the believer. 'Believe, and you have eaten already.'[77] Thus faith enables 'a man to eat that meat and drink that drink, to dwell in Christ, and to have Christ dwelling in him'.[78]

Sacrifice

It is by achieving unity with Christ in his Body that redemption comes. But 'the eucharist is there to keep the Church in mind of her sacrificial character'.[79] The Christ with whom believers are joined is the dying and rising Christ. It is this that is signified in the eucharist. 'The whole redeemed community . . . is offered to God as a universal sacrifice, through the great Priest who offered himself in his suffering for us—so that we might be the body of so great a head—under "the form of a servant". . . . This is the sacrifice which the Church continually celebrates in the sacrament of the altar, a sacrament well-known to the faithful where it is shown to the Church that she herself is offered in the offering which she presents to God.'[80] A purely realist view will not do. What can we make of Augustine's often quoted words : 'If you are the Body of Christ and his members, it is the sacrament of yourselves that is set upon the Lord's table, the sacrament of yourselves that you receive. Be what you receive, and receive what you are'?[81] This cannot stand alongside a realist view. Augustine must mean that the eucharist is the point where the Christian becomes identified with the death and resurrection of Christ. 'The virtue which is apprehended there, is unity, that gathered together into his body, and made his members, we may be what we receive.'[82] We become renewed in the image of Christ.

The idea that one event in time can unite a person with another event in time is hard to grasp. For Augustine it depended on his view that all time is created by God and forms the structure within which man experiences God. God, who lies beyond temporal events, may choose certain events through which to disclose himself and provide other events that enable a connection to be made in man's historical experience. Augustine sees the central event of God's disclosure as the death and resurrection of Christ. He sees the sacraments as God's method of bridging the temporal gap involved in the structure of history he has given to the world. So the Old Testament sacrifices—which he calls sacraments[83]—'present' and 'prefigure' the sacrifice of Christ, just as Christian sacraments 'represent' and 're-figure' the Cross.[84] 'Before the coming of Christ, the flesh and blood of this sacrifice were foreshadowed in the animals slain; in the passion of Christ the types were fulfilled by the true sacrifice; after the ascension of Christ, this sacrifice is commemorated in the sacrament.'[85] The eucharist is not a recollection of something in fact absent. On the Cross Christ was 'himself making the offering, and the oblation. This is the reality, and he intended

the daily sacrifice of the Church to be the sacramental symbol
of this; for the Church, being the body of which he is the head,
learns to offer itself through him.'[86] In the mind, man is able to
transcend intervals of time. 'Once was Christ sacrificed for us . . .
but now there are remnants of thought, when we remember
who has come to us, and what he has forgiven us; by means of
the memory herself, he is daily so sacrificed for us, as if he were
daily renewing us.'[87]

Yet it is not just an activity of the mind that unites the believer
with the sacrifice of Christ. That which brings the fruits of redemption is the humility Christ learnt in order to make himself
a sacrifice. Christ 'gave his Supper, he gave his Passion: he is
filled, who imitates it. The poor imitated it: for they so suffered
as to follow Christ's footsteps.'[88] In so far as the Holy Spirit
creates humility in the believer, as he opens his hands to receive
bread and wine, a man is joining Christ for whom humility led
to sacrifice. Association with the 'humiliation of God' gives birth
to a faith enabling a man to 'be healed from all pride and
haughtiness'.[89] Because the Cross sets before us God taking our
humanity and the form of a servant, so this that we see in the
eucharist 'admonishes us and fits us by faith to be nourished
sacramentally like the angels'.[90] Augustine paraphrased the words
of Christ in John 6 : 57 : 'My emptying of myself effected that I
should live by the Father; that is, should refer my life to him
as the greater; but that any should live by me is effected by that
participation in which he eats me. Therefore, I being humbled,
do live by the Father. Man being raised up, lives by me.'[91] The
fact that the eucharist relates a believer to the Passion of Christ
that happened in a different time makes it possible for Augustine
also to give highly eschatological references to his sacramental
theology. The Christian not only associates himself with a past
event, he is drawn into the whole process of redemption, moving
towards the final City of God. The eucharist is 'daily bread'—
the food we need until we have 'come to Christ himself, and
begun to reign with him for ever'.[92]

At one level Augustine's theology of the eucharist can seem
to be dependent on the Neoplatonic structure with which he
works. Material and temporal things are used in such a way as
to enable man to transcend the material and temporal and come

in touch with the immaterial and eternal. Probably Prenter is right in concluding that Augustine's metaphysical system predominates in his total scheme at the expense of eschatology.[93] But he is right too to point out that for Augustine the eucharist was always pointing forward to the final completion of salvation beyond history. 'The two sacraments of Baptism and Eucharist consist of elements and actions belonging to the order of creation. But through their institution by Christ they are taken into the economy of redemption, they unite the Church on pilgrimage on this earth with her risen and glorified Lord. They have an eschatological function. They point forward to the coming of the Kingdom in its full glory.'[94]

For Augustine the eucharist was not a liturgical code, from which could be read off good doctrine. He would not separate the action from what it signified.[95] In doing so he was nearer to the earlier concept of mystery than he was to Ambrose or the realist tradition that developed in the West. He is near to anyone who will approach the eucharist as an art-form—becoming involved in it and changed by it, as it resonates with different parts of our imagination and experience, and calls out the surprises, which are our experiences of grace, of insight and growth that we had not thought possible.

The problem for us today is that the Platonic framework Augustine used to integrate his sacramental theology is not 'good currency' for people generally. The process of secularization has made its mark. We are not bound to the metaphysics current in the early Church. But we have not found anything as a replacement that can do what Augustine achieved—at least not in conceptual terms. What we do witness today is a resurgence of confidence in the power of ritual forms. J. G. Davies gives a number of examples of 'Secular Rituals'[96] in which people felt compelled to replace a prosaic action with a complex ritual in order to do justice to the depth of significance the action had for them. Harvey Cox, writing about this aspect of modern life, draws particular attention to the way in which 'festivity' enables man to appropriate 'an extended area of life, including the past, into his own experience',[97] thus enlarging his experience and reducing his provincialism. The eucharistic feast has this quality. It also has, as Geoffrey Wainwright has admirably shown, a reference forward to those events that are not yet, but which control the life of the one who hopes for them.[98] Davies indicates the way in which a view of the sacraments might be developed, based upon a serious appreciation of modern attitudes to ritual.[99]

In the present situation the pastor has a responsibility for helping people to appreciate the sacraments by building situations in which they can perceive the power of symbols to have more than immediate reference. Sometimes he will build such situations deliberately, as, for instance in an experimental form of worship in which a number of not normally related things are brought into juxtaposition in such a way that, what I. T. Ramsey called, a 'disclosure situation'[100] may occur. More often the situations will be built by his normal activities becoming parables of the total scheme of reference within which he works. The deeply depressed person visited time after time will suddenly ask : Why do you bother about me? The zealous pastor may be tempted to give an answer. More sensitively he may allow the parable he is enacting to remain without commentary—to make disclosure possible. As we create parallel experiences to the sacramental rituals it will be possible to see that the sacraments, far from being remnants of previous Christian tradition, are in fact the proper vehicles through which an incarnational religion must express itself.

NOTES

1 cf. E. G. Rupp, *Patterns of Reformation* (London, 1969) 25
2 E. Heller, *The Hazard of Modern Poetry* (Cambridge, 1953) 11f.; quoted in S. H. Miller, *The Dilemma of Modern Belief* (London, 1964) 4
3 V. E. Frankl, *The Doctor and the Soul. An Introduction to Logotherapy* (New York, 1955) 47
4 E. J. Tinsley, The Imitation of God in Christ (London, 1960) 21
5 G. Bornkamm in *Theological Dictionary of the New Testament*, ed. G. Kittel (Michigan, 1967) IV 826f.
6 cf. C. W. Dugmore, 'Sacrament and Sacrifice in the Early Fathers' in *Journal of Ecclesiastical History* II, 1951, 26
7 Adv. Marc. iii 19; 229
8 De orat. 19; 25
9 cf. J. H. Srawley, *St Ambrose on the Sacrament and on the*

Mysteries (London, 1950) 37; F. Holmes Dudden, *The Life and Times of St Ambrose* (Oxford, 1935) II 644f.

10 Cat. XXIII 7; 275

11 Or. Cat. XXXVII; 111

12 De myst. ix 58; 150

13 De myst. ix 52–4; 146–8

14 cf. Dudden, op. cit., II 556

15 1 Clem. xii; 49

16 cf. R. A. Markus, 'St Augustine on Signs' in *Phronesis* II, 1957, 64

17 ibid.

18 Enneads VI 2.5; 844

19 De mag. 40; 96f.

20 De mag. 46; cf. Gilson, op. cit., 66f.

21 Retr. I xii; LCC VI 64

22 De mag. 46; 100

23 De doct. chr. II i 1; 34

24 De doct. chr. II i 2; 34

25 De doct. chr. II ii 3; 34f.

26 Markus, op. cit. (Signs), 73

27 De Trin. XV 20; 146

28 cf. R. A. Markus, *Saeculum: History and Society in the Theology of St Augustine* (Cambridge, 1970) 183f. The nearest Augustine gets is in C.D. XV 2.

29 *Christ the Sacrament* (London, 1971)

30 Ep. 54.1; I 197—also De doct. chr. III xix 13; 87 and De vera rel. xvii 33; 240f.

31 H.—M. Feret, 'Sacramentum—Res' in *Revue des sciences philosophie et théologie* 29, 1940, 220

32 R. Prenter, 'Metaphysics and Eschatology in the Sacramental Teaching of St Augustine' in *Studia Theologica* I 1–2, 1948, 8

33 En. in Ps. 58.1; III 127; cf. M. Pontet, *L'Exégèse de S Augustin Prédicateur* (Aubier, 1945) 272f.

34 Ep. 55.13; I 215

35 Ep. 54.1; I 197

36 cf. Van Der Meer, op. cit., 277f.

37 C. Faust. xix 13–14; 244

38 E. Portalié, *A Guide to the Thought of St Augustine* (London, 1960) 246f.; cf. also J. B. Bernardin in *A Companion to the Study of St Augustine* (New York, 1955) ed. R. W. Battenhouse, 6of.

39 Ep. 54.1; I 197

40 C.D. XIV 28; 593
41 Serm. 113.2; I 267
42 De peccat. merit. et remiss. I xx 28; 25
43 cf. G. Wainwright, *Eucharist and Eschatology* (London, 1971) 116f.
44 cf. S. J. Grabowski, op. cit., 181
45 cf. E. C. Whitaker, *Documents of the Baptismal Liturgy* (London, 1960) 92f.
46 Serm. (Miscellanea Agostiniana II 30; 6–19); Whitaker, op. cit., 96
47 De cat. rud. xx 34; 224
48 Tr. in Jo. Ev. XV 4; I 211
49 cf. Van Der Meer, op. cit., 347f.
50 Ep. 185.23; Dods, *On the Donatist Controversy* 499
51 De bapt. V i 1; 479
52 Ep. 33.4; I 61
53 ibid.; I 60
54 cf. N. M. Haring, 'St Augustine's Use of the Word *Character*' in *Mediaeval Studies* XIV, 1952, 80
55 Ep. 185.43; Dods, *On the Donatist Controversy* 513
56 Tr. in Jo. Ev. VI 14; I 83
57 De peccat. merit. et remiss. I xix 24; 24
58 De nupt. et concup. I xx 22; 273
59 De peccat. merit. et remiss. I xxvi 39; 30
60 Serm. 115.4; I 479
61 Serm. 174.9; II 896
62 Prenter, op. cit., 15
63 Tr. in Jo. Ev. LXXX 3; II 300
64 De doct. chr. III ix 13; 87
65 Prenter, op. cit., 18f.
66 De peccat. merit. et remiss. I xxv 38; 30
67 Ep. 98.2; II 15–16
68 cf. E. R. Fairweather, 'St Augustine's Interpretation of Infant Baptism' in *Augustinus Magister*, Communications II (Paris, 1954) 903
69 Romans 6:5; cf. Enchir. xiv 52; 370
70 J. N. D. Kelly, op. cit., 446
71 op. cit., 247f.
72 Ep. 54.1; I 197
73 C. Faust. xix 20; 190
74 Serm. 227; A. G. Hebert, *Liturgy and Society* (London, 1935) 85

75 En. in Ps. 98.9; IV 454
76 Tr. in Jo. Ev. XXVI 12; I 376
77 Tr. in Jo. Ev. XXV 12; I 358
78 Tr. in Jo. Ev. XXVI 18; I 379—cf. Dugmore, op. cit., 31f.
79 Burnaby, op. cit., 124
80 C.D. X 6; 380
81 Serm. 272; Burnaby, op. cit., 124–5
82 Serm. 57.7; I 85
83 cf. C.D. X 5; 377
84 cf. Dugmore, op. cit., 31
85 C. Faust. xx 21; 262
86 C.D. X 20; 401
87 En. in Ps. 75.15; IV 17
88 En. in Ps. 23.27; I 160
89 En. in Ps. 23.27; I 160
90 De lib, arb. III x 30; 190
91 Tr. in Jo. Ev. XXVI 19; I 380
92 Serm. 57.7; I 85
93 op. cit., 20
94 Prenter, op. cit., 10
95 cf. Van Der Meer, op. cit., 311; cf. also F. Van Der Meer, 'Sacramentum chez St Augustin' in *La Maison-Dieu*, 13, 1948, 62
96 *Every Day God* (London, 1973) 307f.
97 *The Feast of Fools* (Cambridge, Mass., 1969) 7
98 op. cit.
99 op. cit., 337f.
100 *Religious Language* (London, 1957)

CHAPTER FOUR

On Creation

AUGUSTINE understood very clearly the need people have for a coherent world-view that creates a framework within which questions of meaning can be handled. One of the most difficult areas for the Christian theologian in the transition from Hebrew to Greek ways of thinking was the doctrine of creation. By the time of Augustine this plank was still missing in the platform built by earlier theologians. Without it a coherent view of the world was not possible and it was for this reason, among others, that creation had more than a peripheral interest for Augustine.

A glance at the text-books on early Christian doctrine would suggest that the crucial themes with which the early Church concerned itself, as it formed its doctrine for preaching in the pagan world, were Christological. This perspective can be justified by abundant references to the early Fathers. Christian theologians had a good deal on their side as they approached the Greek mind on these issues. The gospel, as it centred round the person of Christ and his resurrection, was not altogether 'foolishness' to the Greek. There were models in his culture that could be modified to evoke the concept the Christian believed in. When the Christian theologian came to interpret the Christian doctrine of creation he faced a quite different situation and a much harder task. 'The Greek mind was firmly addicted to the conception of an Eternal Cosmos, permanent and immutable in its essential structure.'[1] To talk about its origin or beginning was strange. The biblical view of creation was alien and unintelligible to the Greek mind. It is not surprising to find that it is speculative theologians such as Origen, Athanasius and Augustine who gave their attention to this problem.

First attempts
Most of the other Fathers seemed content to repeat the orthodoxies of the Christian tradition. For example, Irenaeus writes: 'This is the drawing-up of our faith, the foundation of the build-

ing, and the consolidation of our way of life: God, the Father, uncreated, beyond grasp, invisible; one God the maker of all; this is the first and foremost article of our faith.'[2] What he is doing is merely presenting the view of God that he found in the biblical revelation and is, in particular, influenced by the view of Isaiah 'that God is an all-glorious and all-powerful transcendent Being, the Creator and Lord of all'.[3] E. Frank expressed the problem the Fathers faced: 'The Christian philosophers were fully aware of the fact that their idea of creation, just as their idea of God, was based on their religious faith, on revelation, not on intellectual reasoning. No matter how earnestly they tried to find a philosophical justification for their religious creed, the creation of the world remained a mystery beyond human understanding, the miracle of all miracles'.[4] Some of the Fathers were content to leave it at this point, others felt compelled to examine the concept of creation at greater depth because they saw it as one of the crucial issues upon which depended the Church's success in making its message intelligible in a world dominated by Greek categories of thought.

The Bible presented Christians with a picture of a world entirely contingent upon God's creative act and of a God who is free to act or not. The picture could be translated into Greek terms, but this is a hazardous undertaking, for care had to be exercised to guard against the corruption of the vision by the existing overtones of the categories used to describe it. Origen gives us a good example of this. In his apologetic writing he attempted to present Christianity as something intellectually respectable. He showed how 'he himself, in his own mind, could be satisfied that Christianity was not an irrational credulity but a profound philosophy'.[5] In his presentation Origen emphasized the idea that God could never have become anything that he had not always been. God exercised an 'all-ruling' quality at every moment of his existence. By speaking in this way he was also compelled to speak of the eternal existence of the world, which was intelligible to the Greek mind but at odds with the biblical picture of creation. 'We cannot even call God Almighty if there are none over whom he can exercise his power. Accordingly, to prove that God is almighty we must assume the existence of the universe. For if anyone would have it that certain ages, or periods of time, or whatever he cares to call them, elapsed during which the present creation did not exist, he would undoubtedly prove that in those ages or periods God was not almighty, but that he afterwards became almighty from the time when he began to have creatures over whom he could exercise power.'[6] It is clear that a more adequate reformulation of the biblical idea needed further consideration.

Athanasius believed that the questions about a doctrine of creation could be handled properly by using a distinction between 'essence' and 'powers' and so 'discriminate strictly between the inner Being of God and His creative and "providential" manifestation *ad extra*'.[7] Quite outside the temporal process Christ existed in relationship to the Father. 'For although the Father had never been disposed to create the world or any part of it, yet still the Son would have been with the Father, and the Father in the Son.'[8] Yet God had the power to create and be present in the universe. 'In creation He is present everywhere, yet is distinct in being from it; ordering, directing, giving life to all, containing all, yet is He Himself the Uncontained, existing solely in His Father.'[9] Athanasius is saying that one has to use one way of describing the nature of the Godhead and another for indicating the power of his nature being exercised outside itself. The link is in God's choice or will. God chooses to exercise power and the character of his essence gives him freedom to do this. 'The Divine nature has its power of will, and the energy of this power is productive of the essences of all created beings . . . the creature's existence is altogether external to the substance of the Divine nature, and was imparted only by an act of God's will.'[10] The two modes of existence—that of God's existence and that of creatures—are incomparable. They are related in that God chooses to give existence to creatures.[11] Athanasius was using all his sophistication to present a doctrine that was faithful to the Bible and yet took seriously the objections that could be directed to it by the Greek mind. His solution was to point to a distinction that must be drawn if creation was to be discussed with seriousness. He did not leave the biblical picture as a boulder over which the Greeks had to fall, nor did he hellenize out of recognition the biblical picture. He clarified the issues and set the stage for further discussion.

AUGUSTINE AND CREATION

When we move from the writings of Origen and Athanasius on creation to those of Augustine we enter a subtly different world. He did not work at the white heat of Origen and he did not have the Arians breathing down his neck. He certainly had his own controversies to deal with, that called from him the sort of intensity we find in Origen and Athanasius, but these were connected only marginally with the doctrine of creation. Disputing with the Manichaeans or interpreting Christian doctrine in Neoplatonic language was a more leisurely occupation and this colours the mood of his writing. This is not to say that he lacked any intensity of interest. Three time Augustine attempted to comment on the first three chapters of Genesis: *De Genesi contra Manichaeos* (388–9); *De Genesi ad litteram imperfectus liber* (393–4); *De Genesi ad litteram* (401–15). He gives up the major part of books XI–XIII of the *Confessions* and books XI–XII of the *City of God* to various aspects of this subject, as well as making reference to it in a host of other works. Why did this subject dominate his mind so strongly? Partly because, like Origen and Athanasius, he saw creation as a fundamental theological problem that demanded the application of his analytical and speculative powers. But with Augustine there is another important element. When the biblical view of creation is taken seriously the Christian cannot treat it wholly as a subject for detached cerebration. It confronts man with questions concerning his own identity and his relations with the world. Theology can so easily be mesmerized by ideas. Over these we have some control. Actual relationships with people and things are much more difficult.

We have sufficient evidence of a conflict in Augustine between the power of his mind and his inability to deal with personal situations. We are given in the *Confessions* a catena of incidents: the death of his close friend while he was teaching at Tagaste[12] plunged Augustine into the depths of misery from which he sought to escape by moving to Carthage; he was attracted to leave for Rome because he 'had been informed that the students there studied more quietly and were better kept under the control of stern discipline'[13] than at Carthage where 'there was a shameful and intemperate licence among the students'[14]—and also, one suspects, to break the control his mother, Monica, was exercising over him; at Rome his students evaded 'paying their master's fees'[15] and so he moved to Milan. What he could not control he avoided. The problem that delayed Augustine's conversion concerned actions not ideas. Immediately before the episode in the garden at Milan Augustine said to Alypius: 'What is the matter with us?. . . The uninstructed start up and take heaven, and we—with all our learning but so little heart—see where we wallow in flesh and blood'.[16] Again his intellect was proving insufficient and as he moved into the garden it was a battle of the will, not the mind, that went on. 'It was I who willed and it was also I who was unwilling. In either case, it was I. I neither willed with my whole will nor was I wholly unwilling. And so I was at war with myself and torn apart by myself.'[17] In all these experiences Augustine found himself having to come to terms with parts of himself, other than his intellect, and to relate himself to the concrete problems of living. Augustine's call to pastoral responsibilities in the Church repeated in him the same tension. After leaving Italy he settled at Tagaste with a few friends determined to form a 'religious college'[18] devoted to learning and holiness. Then came the call to the priesthood in Hippo and his dream of a life of detachment was destroyed. He now had to face responsibilities that were uncongenial to him and, characteristically, he devoted the rest of his life fully to them. It is against this background that we have to see Augustine's obsession with creation. In the world of the intellect he lived at ease. It was his relationships to the world that formed the problem. And it is his struggle to work through this inner tension that we see expressed in his writings on creation. What was so vividly important to Augustine as a man was an issue of perennial importance. He is a pastor offering his own solution in the hope that it may be helpful to others.

Platonic foundation

The link between God and the world is, in Gilson's phrase, 'a relationship of similarity'.[19] Augustine took the Platonic doctrine of 'ideas' as his starting point. 'The ideas are, in effect, radical forms or essential expressions of things, fixed and immutable,

not formed of themselves, and by that, eternal and permanent in
their mode of being, linked together in the divine intelligence.'[20]
The world of creatures is a reflection of certain ideas in the mind
of God. 'God, therefore, knew all things which He made before
He made them. ... He knew them, therefore, as things to be
made, not as things made; He knew them that He might make
them, not because He had made them. Hence although they were
already known, for except by one knowing them they could not
be made, yet those things, which were known that they might be
made, did not begin to be until after they were made; and that
they might be rightly made, were known before they were
made.'[21] Things exist by participation in the ideas or patterns
in the mind of God.[22] 'It is by participation that all exists which
does exist, in whatever way it is.'[23] The world thus comes into
being when God gives expression to the already existing ideas
within his own being. In this way Augustine makes clear that
all creatures have their origin in God. They have no right to
existence of their own. All they have is a resemblance of God. A
creature bears the 'similitude of him from whom it has received
existence'.[24]

The sequence of creation

Though in this way Augustine links together God and his
creation, the distance between them is a vast chasm. Was it
possible to reduce the sense of distance without destroying the
distinction? Augustine attempted this by describing 'stages' in
God's creative act. For himself, though not necessarily convinc-
ingly for us, he found in Genesis a clue. God created 'heaven and
earth'. Both heaven and earth must be seen as objects of God's
creation. Heaven is *the house of God*. 'It is not an earthly house
and it is not made from any celestial matter; but it is a spiritual
house, and it partakes in thy eternity because it is without blemish
forever. ... Still, it is not coeternal with thee, O God, since it is
not without beginning—it was created.'[25] It is 'a certain sublime
created order which cleaves with such a chaste love to the true
and truly eternal God that, although it is not coeternal with him,
yet it does not separate itself from him, and does not flow away
into any mutation of change or process but abides in true contemplation of him alone'.[26] So heaven, though a creature, is more

like God and less like earth. Though this conception owes much
to Plotinus, the use of a phrase such as 'chaste love' may indicate
that in his approach to creation Augustine is expressing some of
his own sexual conflicts. He does not seem to have resolved
adequately the normal oedipal tensions of growing to maturity.
It may be that he needed a feminine element in his doctrine to
compensate for the inevitable creative, father-like, role of God.
This he gives himself in his doctrine of heaven.[27]

Along with heaven earth was created. As we shall see,
Augustine believed that everything was created simultaneously,
but also recognized that a non-sequential picture of creation is
difficult for the human imagination and so he analyses out the
causal sequence in creation that must not be understood as a
time-sequence. First in the causal sequence, God created unformed matter. 'I hear thy Scripture saying, "In the beginning
God made the heaven and the earth, but the earth was invisible
and unformed, and darkness was over the abyss" . . . by invisible
and unformed earth, I understood that which suffers no temporal
vicissitude.'[28] This unformed matter is the lowest element in
creation—'near to nothing'[29]—is what the 'ancients' called 'Hyle'.
'By "Hyle" I mean matter completely without form and quality,
out of which are formed the qualities we perceive. . . . It has no
form by which we can perceive it. Indeed, it can hardly be
conceived because it is so utterly without form. But it has the
capacity to receive form.'[30] From this 'invisible and unformed'
matter God created 'visible and composite forms'. These material
forms exist in two kinds. There are those whose form was fixed
at their creation and there are those which were created with
a capacity to develop subsequently to their creation. 'When the
day of creation came, not only the sun and the moon and the
stars, whose species remain in their rotary motion, and the earth
and the deeps, which suffer changing movements, and joined
together below produce the other part of the world; but also
those things which earth and water produced potentially and
causally, before in the course of time they came into being in
the shape in which they are now known to us.'[31] It is by intro-
ducing this distinction that Augustine is able to hold together
the assertion that God created all things simultaneously and the
fact that in the process of time we see new things appearing. So

we have things that were created and have remained essentially the same, and things that have developed from what he calls *rationes causales* or *rationes seminales*.[32] If Augustine had been writing today he would have used probably the illustration of the programming of a computer. The moment the computer receives its programme all its subsequent computations are determined and controlled by that initial programme. Instead, he uses the picture of a tree, which develops in the course of time from its beginning in a seed. 'Just as in that seed there were together invisibly all the things which would develop into the tree, so the world itself is to be thought to have had together—since God created all things together—all the things which were made in it and with it.'[33] In another place he used the metaphor of pregnancy: 'That which is created may come forth into being at this time or that, and in this way or that way. For all these things . . . have already been created in a kind of texture of the elements, but they come forth when they get opportunity. For as mothers are pregnant with young, so the world itself is pregnant with the causes of things that are born; which are not created in it, except from that highest essence, where nothing either springs up or dies, either begins to be or ceases. But the applying from without of adventitious causes, which, although they are not natural, yet are to be applied according to nature, in order that those things which are contained and hidden in the secret bosom of nature may break forth and be outwardly created in some way by the unfolding of the proper measures and numbers and weights they have received in secret from him "who has ordained all things in measure and number and weight".'[34] As Gilson points out, the Augustinian doctrine of seminal reasons is developed to show that what things appear to be new are not really new at all, for their 'newness' was already contained, though hidden, within them.[35]

Hierarchy in creation

Speculation about the act of creation and the nature of the relation between the creature and the creating God is an important part of the theological task, responding as it does to man's curiosity about beginnings and relationships. But man living within creation is faced with a world to be explored. Though

Augustine was not a scientific man in the modern sense he did attempt to analyse the features of the created world and displayed a highly developed observational power, even though he was, like his contemporaries, open to a certain credulity about some alleged physical events.[36]

Augustine observing the world of creatures saw its structure as hierarchical.[37] 'God is existence in a supreme degree—he supremely is—and he is therefore immutable. Hence he gave existence to the creatures he made out of nothing; but it was not his own supreme existence. To some he gave existence in a higher degree, to some in a lower, and thus he arranged a scale of existences of various natures.'[38] This hierarchical structure may be described in terms of existence, life and knowledge. 'To exist, to live and to know are three things. A stone exists but does not live. An animal lives but has not intelligence. But he who has intelligence most certainly both exists and lives. Hence I do not hesitate to judge that that is more excellent, which has all these qualities than that in which one or both of them is absent.'[39] One further distinction is possible. Both plants and animals live, but animals have the facility, shared with man, of sensory perception. God has given man the 'existence (he shares) with stones . . . the life of the senses he shares with animals, and the life of the intellect, shared only with the angels'.[40]

It is in keeping with the general attitude towards creation that we have noted that Augustine could not leave his reflections at this point. He is a little like the irritating preachers with whom companionship is often marred by their persistent observation of sermon illustrations in whatever happens. This hierarchical structure in creation must tell him something about God. Romans 1:20 and Wisdom 13:1f invited him to regard creation in this way.[41] What Lyttkens calls Augustine's dualism of ideas and things[42] prevents him from being faithful to the point Paul was making in Romans 1:20. He follows the road and then pulls off it. 'I do not travel very far for examples, when I mean to give you some similitude to your God from your own mind; because surely not in the body, but in that same mind, was man made after the image of God. Let us seek God in his own similitude; let us recognise the Creator in his own image.'[43] Ideas

Augustine can tolerate, but things cannot be brought too close to God who can only be conceived of in purely spiritual terms.

'Texts can easily be cited in which empirical knowledge is slightly spoken of.'[44] Nevertheless Augustine had great interest in the matter-of-fact things. For example, he describes the structure of the brain: 'It has three ventricles: an anterior one, whence all feeling; another behind, at the neck, whence all motion; a third between the above two, and here memory dwells' and adds that 'knowledge of these facts is due to the discovery that injuries to those various parts result respectively in loss of feeling, movement or memory'.[45] He describes himself watching with intense interest 'a lizard catching flies, or a spider entangling them as they fly into her webs'.[46] He was prepared to make experiments to test out alleged features of the natural world that he found hard to believe and describes an experiment on the corruptibility of the flesh of the peacock.[47] He also warns Christians against clinging to crude beliefs about the natural world on the authority of Scripture.[48] Scattered throughout his writings we find that Augustine's curiosity about the natural world has produced a detailed account of a whole range of subjects concerned with animals, birds, insects and reptiles.[49] As we have suggested above, for Augustine it was the abstractions that connected with nature that provoked his theological, as opposed to human, interest. The order, beauty and goodness of the natural world fascinated him.

Order

Though Augustine's curiosity often fastened on the strange and unusual in nature,[50] the normal orderliness of the world impressed him most. So to Faustus he says: 'Looking at the flesh itself, do we not see in the construction of its vital parts, in the symmetry of form, in the position and arrangement of the limbs of action and the organs of sensation, all acting in harmony; do we not see in the adjustment of measures, in the proportion of numbers, in the order of weights, the handiwork of the true God?'[51] The predictions of astronomic calculation seem to have been particularly impressive to him.[52] He was not blind to elements in the world that appeared to disrupt its harmony, but even here he claimed that this appearance is only because we cannot perceive the world as a whole 'in which these small parts, which are to us so disagreeable, fit together to make a scheme of ordered beauty'.[53] Nature as a whole he describes in the following way: 'The whole process of nature ... involves certain natural laws of its own, according to which the spirit of life, which is a creature, gives expression to its own definite urges, determined in a certain way.... And the elements of this corporeal world have each their specific power and quality, determining what each may or may not do, and what each may or may not become.'[54] As Cochrane points out[55] this view makes the Greek idea of 'chance' as being an essential part of creation 'a mere illusion of classical idealism' and also rules out the possibility of their being any antinomy between Creator and creation. Here again the Stoic and Neoplatonic idea of *seminal reasons* is used to explain, this time, how within an ordered universe miracles, that seem to be a violation of this order, occur. God sends rain, thunder and lightning, 'draws up the sap through the roots of the vine to the bunch of grapes and makes wine' in the ordinary course of events, but he is also able to give rain at the prayer of Elijah, thunder and lightning at Sinai and wine at Cana in an unusual manner so that 'certain intimations were given by them'.[56] All this is because *invisible seeds* are implanted within nature that permit unusual events.[57] So Augustine can define a miracle as something 'not contrary to nature, but contrary to what is known of nature',[58] for 'God, the Author and Creator of all natures, does nothing contrary to nature; for whatever is done by him who appoints all natural order and measure and proportion must be natural in every case'.[59] Over against the Ciceronian ascription of apparently miraculous events to chance[60] and Jerome who saw miracles as 'a revelation of the power of a personal God to control the vagaries of an impersonal Fate'[61] Augustine emphasized the ultimate dependence of all things upon God who gave to nature order, whether that order can be clearly seen or is hidden.

Beauty

When Augustine saw order he also saw beauty. In this he stood in the Hellenic tradition. Before his conversion, in his first work[62] he wrote *On the Fair and the Fit*, but this general interest in

beauty was later to be part of his doctrine of participation. The
source of beauty is in God and things that are created bear
resemblance to the beauty of God.[63] When this beauty of
creatures is recognized by us it is because the laws of beauty are
implanted in us as part of God's creative act. 'Whatever delights
you in corporeal objects and entices you by appeal to the bodily
senses, you may see is governed by number, and when you ask
how that is so, you will return to your mind within, and know
that you could neither approve nor disapprove things of sense
unless you had within you, as it were, laws of beauty by which
you judge all beautiful things which you perceive in the world.'[64]
This view connects with Augustine's epistemology expounded in
De Magistro where Christ is seen as the 'inward Teacher', the
one who implants the notion of beauty within us so that we are
able to recognize the beautiful in what is external to us. Like the
Platonists,[65] Augustine 'sought to transmute aesthetic experience
and express it in terms of purely rational experience'.[66] 'In his
early work on music he seeks to give a scientific interpretation of
music by a theory of rhythm and intervals; this provided a kind
of key to principles of harmony, which could be mathematically
deduced and which, in their turn, were a reflection of the cosmic
harmony of the spheres. None of this, however, had the least
connection with singing or playing or with instruments or composition.'[67] We have already noticed this tendency in Augustine
to rationalize experience. It seems an example of the intellectual
defence of a schizoid personality.

Sometimes Augustine's lack of interest in art for art's sake
enabled him to get straight to the heart of things. As when he
was preaching at the consecration of a new basilica he refused
to comment on the architecture and turned from 'the dead stones
to the living congregation'.[68] But one longs to read 'I raise my
eyes to Heaven, to the beauty of the stars; I behold with wonder
the brightness of the sun, sufficing to the bringing forth of the
day, the moon cheering the darkness of the night'[69] without
Augustine having to add 'I thirst for him who made them'. Pious
and right as such a sentiment is, we cannot but feel he is somehow defending himself against ordinary human experience. The
same sense we get when he takes another tack and allegorizes the
sun as Christ, the moon as the Church and the heavens as the

Apostles.[70] Fortunately there were occasions when his defences went down and we see that a claim that Augustine was a man of poetic sensibility is justified. In Augustine's case this is when he relaxes his intellect and allows his whole person to respond to life and the God he finds within it. We see the two aspects of this tension in which Augustine lived in a passage in the *Confessions*: 'What is it that I love in loving thee? Not physical beauty, nor the splendour of time, nor the radiance of the light— so pleasant to our eyes—not the sweet melodies of the various kind of songs, nor the fragrant smell of flowers and ointments and spices; not manna and honey, not the limbs embraced in physical love—it is not these I love when I love my God. Yet it is true that I love a certain kind of light and sound and fragrance and food and embrace in loving my God, who is the light and sound and fragrance and food and embracement of my inner man—where that light shines into my soul which no place can contain, where time does not snatch away the lovely sound, where no breeze disperses the sweet fragrance, where no eating diminishes the food there provided, and where there is an embrace that no satiety comes to sunder. This is what I love when I love my God.'[71] The God whom he loved drew him, if a little hesitatingly, into a certain love of what he had created.

Goodness

If things exist by participation in God, then the one quality above all others that belongs to them must be goodness, for 'the Supreme Good beyond all others is God'.[72] It seemed self-evident to Augustine 'that the goodness of God, (led) to the creation of good'.[73] He found it difficult to understand why the Manichaeans[74] or even Origen[75] had to suppose that the goodness of the world was necessary to repulse 'the evil that fought against (God)'.[76] With simplicity he describes the parts that make up the world and concludes: 'These things we see, and each of them is good; and the whole is very good!'[77] Augustine had a certain *joie de vivre* giving 'to the conscious love of life an intensity and force much greater than the modern temper is disposed to allow'.[78] Simply to enjoy the goodness of living is a prize to be cherished. 'Those who are wretched are for this very reason unwilling to die. ... If those wretches were offered immortality, on the condition that their misery would be undying, with the alternative that if they refused to live for ever in the same misery they would cease to have any existence at all, and would perish utterly, then they would certainly be overjoyed to choose perpetual misery in preference to complete annihilation.'[79] By now we should be prepared to expect that no subject can be treated by Augustine with this simplicity. He was not so blind as not to see the existence of evil and somewhere a place in his scheme must be found for it that did not depreciate the fundamental conviction that what God creates is good. This place is provided by regarding evil as an element of non-existence.

As Augustine saw a hierarchical order in the natural world, he also saw degrees of goodness. 'All things are good; better in proportion as they are better measured, formed and ordered, less good where there is less measure, form and order. These three things, measure, form and order . . . are as it were generic good things to be found in all that God has created. Where these three things are present in a high degree there are small goods. And where they are absent there is no goodness. Moreover, where these three things are present in a high degree there are things great by nature. Where they are present in a low degree there are things small by nature. Where they are absent there is no natural thing at all. Therefore, every natural existent is good.'[80] Evil may be used to describe the element of vitiation when the measure, form and order of a thing is diminished. Evil 'is nothing but the corruption of natural measure, form and order. What is called an evil nature is a corrupt nature. . . . It is bad only so far as it is corrupted'.[81] Thus Augustine recognizes the fact of evil things but believes that their evil cannot be abstracted from them as a positive quality. Since evil is a privation of the generic good in all creatures there cannot be anything wholly bad, for if that were the case it would cease to exist. 'The good in created things can be diminished and augmented. For good to be diminished is evil; still, however much it is diminished, something must remain of its original nature as long as it exists at all.'[82] An analogy suggested by T. R. Milford is that of holes in a road.[83] The good road is made bad by pot-holes which are, in a sense, absence of road. There is nothing where road ought to be. So evil is a gap in the goodness of existing things and not, as the Manichaeans thought, a thing itself.

This view of the status of evil bears resemblance to the doctrine of Plotinus,[84] but Bonner warns against over-emphasizing Augustine's debt, for 'the Plotinian Evil is not the simple privation of Augustine's doctrine'.[85] This correction is welcome for so often expositors speak of Augustine's doctrine being 'derived' from Plotinus.[86] It may also be pointed out that Athanasius, at least, gave a hint of the theory Augustine developed: 'Men, having turned from the contemplation of God to evil of their own devising, had come inevitably under the law of death . . . as they had at the beginning come into being out of non-existence, so were they now on the way to returning, through corruption, to non-existence again. The presence and love of the Word had called them into being; inevitably, therefore, when they lost the knowledge of God, they lost existence with it; for it is God alone who exists, evil is non-being, the negation and antithesis of good.'[87]

Time

One further aspect of creation fascinated Augustine, as it has many before and since. Time presents man with a puzzle and places great strains upon his imagination and language. 'From the first dawn of speculation till now, from the time of Parmenides and Zeno to that of Mr Bradley and M. Bergson, there has been no problem that has seemed so baffling as Time.'[88] Augustine well expresses the puzzle in saying: 'What, then, is time? If no one asks me, I know what it is. If I wish to explain it to him who asks me, I do not know.'[89] Nevertheless he felt compelled to discuss time for a number of reasons. First, because it had to be discussed as part of the doctrine of creation he formulated in opposition to the Manichaeans and Neoplatonists.[90] Second, because the polarity of time and eternity echoed other polarities within him that he felt so deeply, such as the 'conflict between the lusts of the flesh and the longing of the soul; the opposition of matter and spirit'.[91] Third, because he saw a man's life within time as being of supreme importance for his ultimate destiny.[92] Fourth, because for Augustine the investigation of time 'is a study in contingency, finiteness, creatureliness, dependence, incompleteness, imperfection—a study of the limitation of being that characterises *any* finite entity, that entity which *is*, but which is not He Who Is'.[93] Being moved by these reasons Augustine gives to us 'the first serious attempt at an account of time in seven centuries, and the last for fourteen more'.[94]

A considerable literature is devoted to the antecedents of Augustine's views of time.[95] Plotinus set out a theory that bears resemblances to that of Augustine, but Green sets out the two schemes and concludes: 'the differences are more impressive than the similarities.'[96] Callahan has argued an interesting case for influence by Basil of Caesarea.[97]

If you state that the world is created you seem to imply that there was a time when the world was not. If you believe in the eternity of the world, as the Manichaeans did, you would want to ask believers in creation what was happening before creation took place and why God chose to create when he did and not before. This sort of question addressed to him by the Manichaeans provoked Augustine's discussion of time in the *Confessions*. He was tempted to answer the question: What was God doing before he made heaven and earth? with the quip: 'He was preparing hell for those who pry too deep.'[98] Instead he launched upon an extensive analysis of the issues that lay behind questions like this. To ask what happened before one event in a sequence of events is meaningful. But to ask what happened before the term 'before' was given meaning by a sequence of events is to raise an unanswerable question. The picture of creation that Augustine presented of God giving creation an absolute beginning required the concept of time itself as a creature. 'Thou madest that very time itself, and periods could not pass by before thou madest the whole temporal procession.'[99] 'Time, in Augustine's view, was a relation between temporal things, in virtue of which they could be said to be before or after one another. It came into being with temporal things, and it makes no sense to speak of time before there were temporal things. He rejected, in effect, his opponents' conception of time as substantial in the way that temporal things are substantial, and as capable of being spoken about in the same language as things and events.'[100] All this is a preliminary clearing of the ground—a dogmatic presentation of that sort of doctrine of creation that includes time as a creature—before he asks the prior and more fundamental question: What is time?

Time is a relationship between temporal things. It has no significance outside the creaturely world. It may be partitioned into past, present and future. It always has direction and is irreversible. 'If we fix on any middle year of this century as present, those before it are past, those after it are future.'[101] This sense of past and future is understood in human experience, but it is not so easy to understand the present. 'One hour . . . passes away in fleeting fractions. The part of it that has fled is past; what remains is still future. If any fraction of time be conceived that cannot now be divided into the most minute momentary point, this alone is what we may call time present. But this flies so rapidly from future to past that it cannot be extended by any delay. For if it is extended, it is then divided into past and future. But the present has no extension whatever.'[102] The existence of the present depends upon its perpetual passing away. If it has length itself it would cease to be the present. As we reflect on the present 'all we are left with is a point without dimension, the point at which the not-yet-real becomes the no-longer-real; and whatever reality it has cannot have duration'.[103] Nevertheless, we are aware of 'intervals of time' and make comparative judgements. 'We measure the passage of time when we measure the intervals of perception.'[104] This is a paradoxical element in our experience for 'who can measure times past which now are no longer, or times future which are not yet . . . while time is passing, it cannot be perceived and measured; but when it is past, it cannot, since it is not'.[105] And since present has no extension it cannot be measured. Later Augustine explodes with the puzzle of it all: 'Does not my soul most truly confess to thee that I do measure intervals of time? But what is it that I thus measure, O my God, and how is it that I do not know that I thus measure?'[106] Augustine refuses to employ the Platonic and Aristotelian idea that the motions of physical bodies in space constitute time, providing us with standard intervals of time.[107] The choice of certain motions, e.g. sun, moon and stars, is purely arbitrary. He concludes that 'time is nothing other than extendedness; but extendedness of what I do not know. . . . The extendedness may be of the mind itself.'[108] Time past, present and future cannot have a substantial existence and so Augustine resorts to a psychological explanation. We are able to measure time because what happens to us makes an impression upon us which remains in our memory even after the event has passed.[109] 'It is in you, O mind of mine, that I measure the periods of time . . . I measure as time present the impression that things make on you as they pass by and what remains after they have passed by—I do not measure the things themselves which have passed by and left their impression on you. This is what I measure when I measure periods of time. Either, then, these are the periods of time or else I do not measure time at all.'[110] We expect something, calling it out of the future, and when it is here our mind considers it and so it passes into our memories. The spacing out of events is done within the mind. 'Future time, which is non-existent, is not long; but "a long future" is "a long expectation of the future". Nor is time past, which is now no longer, long; a "long past" is "a long memory of the past".'[111] Only creatures, possessing minds capable of the distinguishable acts of expectation, attention and memory, can in fact recognize the direction of a flow of events and call it time. Only where there is a creature possessing mind is there the capability of history having meaning, for the rest of nature events are random. Having passed through the intellectual travail of discussing time and come to this conclusion, that is apparently unsatisfying to himself, Augustine breaks into rapturous praise of God: 'who art unchangeably eternal, that is, the truly eternal Creator of minds. As in the beginning thou knewest both the heaven and the earth without any change in thy knowledge, so thou didst make heaven and earth in their beginnings without any division in thy action. Let him who understands this confess to thee.'[112]

Sexuality

The status of created things may be discussed in abstract terms, but it is in attitudes to their use that men reveal their deepest convictions. Man's sexuality is the point where his creatureliness and spirituality have to come to terms with each other or disintegrate. It may be said that a man's doctrine of creation is revealed by his attitude towards sexuality, and probably in the end a man's understanding of sexuality determines his doctrine far more than biblical and dogmatic traditions. We have seen some hint of this already in our exposition of Augustine. As we approach Augustine on marriage and sexuality we need to guard against a temptation to make his exposition a norm that casts doubt upon the integrity of some of his other teaching on creation. We must admit that there is no person who is perfectly integrated and is free from a constant dialogue between different aspects of his nature. We need too to remember the writings of other Christians of the period that indicate views that would be wholly rejected by modern man.

From very early days the Church had expressed very confused attitudes to marriage. Clement of Alexandria well reflects the general confusion. He recognized the opportunity marriage affords for the cultivation of certain virtues that is denied to the unmarried. Somewhat cynically he thinks the unmarried tend to be more selfish and have fewer opportunities for self-denial, but 'the prize in the contest of men is won by him who has trained himself by the discharge of the duties of husband and father and by the supervision of a household, regardless of pleasure and pain—by him, I say, who in the midst of his solicitude for his family shows himself inseparable from the love of God and rises superior to every temptation that assails him through children and wife and servants and possessions'.[113] But he could also maintain that the true Christian gnostic 'circumscribes his desires in reference both to possession and to enjoyment, not exceeding the limit of necessity . . . to such an one, his wife, after conception, is a sister'.[114] Sexual intercourse is a necessity for social reasons, i.e. the maintenance of the human race : 'We must by all means marry, both for our country's sake, for the succession of children, and as far as we are concerned, the perfection of the world.'[115] It ceases to have usefulness for the perfect Christian beyond this necessity. Methodius, in his allegory upon the Feast of Tabernacles, similarly cannot believe that men can 'come to the Feast with Christ if they have not decked their tabernacles with the branches of chastity'.[116] Origen seems to have taken over completely the widespread view of many ancient religions that defilement attaches to the physical contact of sexual relations and his views on marriage express a revolt against creation. The tenor of Clement's views is not so much direct opposition to the creatureliness of man but rather the disturbance sexuality creates in man's inner peace. What he is wanting is for the Christian man, not merely to avoid sexual contact, but to seek freedom from desire. 'Our aim is not that while a man feels desire he should get the better of it, but that he should be continent even respecting desire itself. ... A man who marries for the sake of begetting children must practise continence so that it is not desire he feels for his wife, whom he ought to love, and that he may beget children with a chaste and controlled will.'[117] Here, as Professor Chadwick points out, Clement is appealing to a world-denying strain in New Testament thought which, when it comes into contact with the Hellenistic world, 'meets, so to speak, with a resonant sounding-board upon which the gospel of redemption from sin becomes vastly magnified and filled out to be redemption from this material world, the body, and all the ills that flesh is heir to'.[118]

How does Augustine deal with these questions? He wrote three treatises directly upon marriage: *De Bono Conjugali*; *De Adulterinis Conjugiis*; *De Nuptiis et Concupiscentia*. There he sets out the framework of his thought on the subject, but it is often in passing in other works, particularly those of a directly pastoral nature, that his attitudes are revealed. In his dealings with people on sexual questions he was sensible and realistic. We see him as a man who knows, at least part of, his own sexuality and the strength of sexual impulses. So he is sensitive to the importance of his advice when dealing with such volcanic forces. In his pastoral work as a bishop he was careful to avoid setting a pattern of action which, though he could control it himself, was capable of getting out of hand if his clergy followed it. Thus, odd as it may seem to us, he avoided having even his sister to stay in his house and meeting women except in the presence of others.[119] Epistle 262 gives us Augustine's response to the woman Ecdicia, a married woman who had vowed continence without first consulting her husband. Augustine had declared his approval of married couples making a vow of continence: 'More blessed surely are those marriages to be regarded which, whether after they were attended with the procreation of children or whether in them this earthly offspring has not even been considered, have been able to preserve continence with mutual consent between the parties.'[120] Ecdicia may have expected his approval, but got his condemnation as point by point he showed how her conduct had been wrong. In this letter we have a fine example of a pastor's skill in exploring with the one to whom he ministers the implications of actions and how one can rescue from mistakes a course that holds the possibility of more appropriate relationships with others. 'I have written this to you, since you thought fit to ask my advice, not in order to undermine your righteous design by any words from me, but I am grieved at what your husband has done as a result of your irregular and imprudent conduct. It is your duty most earnestly to think how he may be restored, if your wish to belong to Christ is sincere. Put on therefore humility of mind, and in order that God may help you while you persevere, do not you scorn your husband while he perishes . . .'[121]

In the matter of marriage Augustine's outlook is consistent within his basic treatises on the subject. He began his treatise on *The Good of Marriage* at a point from which he will not retract. Marriage is good because it is part of the social framework of life that God has given. 'Forasmuch as each man is part of the human race, and human nature is something social, and has a great and natural good, the power also of friendship; on this account God willed to create all men out of one, in order that they might be held in their society not only by likeness of kind, but also by bond of kindred. Therefore the first natural bond of human society is man and wife.'[122] We are not to call marriage good because it is better than fornication 'otherwise there will be two evils, of which the second is the worse : or fornication will also be good, because adultery is worse. . . . Therefore marriage and fornication are not two evils, whereof the second is worse : but marriage and continence are two goods, whereof the second is better.'[123] We may compare the good of marriage with other goods, but we cannot deny the goodness of marriage without calling in question the good of the social nature of humanity given by God. This absolute goodness residing in marriage is productive of three blessings : the procreation of children; the bond of mutual love—'a kind of free bondage'; a kindling of the flame of divine love.[124]

What then is the feature of the sexual relationship that creates Augustine's ambivalent attitude towards it? Sexual relationships cannot be separated from concupiscence which 'assumes power not only over the whole body, and not only from the outside, but also internally; it disturbs the whole man, when the mental emotion combines and mingles with the physical craving, resulting in a pleasure surpassing all physical delights. So intense is the pleasure that when it reaches its climax there is an almost total extinction of mental alterness; the intellectual sentries, as it were, are overwhelmed. Now surely any friend of wisdom and holy joys . . . would prefer, if this were possible, to beget children without lusts of this kind. For then the parts created for this task would be servants of his mind, even in their function of procreation, just as the other members are its servants in the various tasks to which they are assigned.'[125] Here we see again Augustine's fear of what cannot be controlled by mind and will. The *imperium* granted to man in Genesis 1:28 was made to extend beyond other creatures, over which man must exercise dominion, to every part of his creatureliness. Although there is some evidence that man can develop certain control over his own involuntary bodily mechanisms it is clear that he is made in such a way that his will has only limited control over his own body. When Augustine speculates[126] on how before the Fall man's generative organs might have been subject to his will, to be fully consistent he would have had to consider how breathing and heart-beat would likewise have been controlled by the will rather than involuntary reflexes. 'For Augustine, the sexual act is never anything but concupiscential. Love has no power to transform it in any significant way; there is no essential difference between the basic biological act of sex and the act of sex which is the physical consummation of a union of hearts and minds. This is the fatal flaw in Augustine's analysis.'[127] When love is binding two people together the suspension of all mental activity in the moment of consummation this 'oblivion marks the loss of the self in something outside of and other than itself'.[128] The climax of human sexuality becomes *in fact* the bond of mutuality—linking the individual within the one essential element in the social framework—regarded by Augustine as the 'great and natural good' of marriage.[129] Augustine was within a hair's-breadth of an insight that would have influenced the whole

course of the Church's teaching on marriage and sexuality. He
was prevented from doing so by seeing good only in that which
he could control.[130]

Conclusion

At almost every point the doctrine of creation which Augustine
developed is inadequate for our purposes today. The metaphysical assumption of the unchangeability of God is called in
question today as an assumption that does not help to bring into
coherence our ways of thinking about God, and 'process
theology' attempts to indicate the way a doctrine of creation
might go, based on other assumptions.[131] The whole question of
the nature of time is under discussion in a way that it has not
been since Augustine's day.[132] Certainly Augustine's view of
sexuality would suffer greatly from modern understanding of the
nature of human sexuality. The way in which he used biblical
materials to support views to which he adhered for extra-biblical
reasons could not be tolerated today.

If there is any value in Augustine's presentation it is that he
gives us a paradigm of how a man approaches with a high sense
of seriousness the task of making the gospel understandable in
terms of current concepts and assumptions. It is the rigour of his
method that teaches us far more than the content of his doctrine.

Today there are additional questions to be answered, but the
questions Augustine faced are still important. In what way can
we relate God to his world in such a fashion that neither is God
completely separated from his world, nor is he inseparable from
it? Does the Christian simply accept the existence of the world
or does he need to have some view of its origins? Are some parts
of creation more important than others? If so, what are the
responsibilities man has for the rest of creation? Is the created
world orderly, beautiful and good? If so, has this any significance? If not, does this matter? What can we make of time?
And how can we understand our sexuality in relation to God?
We could consider these questions because they are interesting
in their own right. They are also questions which, at various
points, have pastoral significance in contributing coherence to
man's search for meaning.

NOTES

1 G. Florovsky, 'The Concept of Creation in St Athanasius' in *Studia Patristica* VI, 1962; cf. H. Lyttkens, 'The Analogy between God and the World' in *Uppsala Universitets Årsskrift* I, 1953, 110

2 Proof of the Apostolic Preaching 6; 51

3 J. Lawson, *The Biblical Theology of St Irenaeus* (London, 1948) 56; cf. Adv. Haer. IV 19.2; 437

4 E. Frank, *Philosophical Understanding and Religious Truth* (Oxford, 1954) 59

5 H. Chadwick, *Origen: Contra Celsum* (Oxford, 1953) ix

6 De princ. I 2.10; 23; cf. J. N. D. Kelly, *Early Christian Creeds* (London, 1950) 137; B. Drewery, *Origen and the Doctrine of Grace* (London, 1960) 68f.

7 Florovsky, op. cit., 47

8 Contra Arianos II 31; 118

9 De incarn. 17; 45

10 Contra Arianos II 2; 84–5; A comparison can be made here with Hartshorne's notion of 'dipolarity', cf. D. A. Pailin, 'A Christian Possibility of Proclaiming the "Death of God"' in *The Church Quarterly*, January 1969, 229.

11 op. cit., 51f.

12 Conf. IV iv 7f.

13 Conf. V viii 14

14 ibid.; 103

15 Conf. V xii 22; 110

16 Conf. VIII viii 19; 170

17 Conf. VIII x 22; 172

18 Bonner, op. cit., 108; cf. Possidius, Vita 3; 196

19 Gilson, op. cit., 210

20 De div. qu. LXXXIII 46.2

21 Ad Orosium viii 9; E. Przywara, *An Augustine Synthesis* (London, 1945) 112

22 cf. Lyttkens, op. cit., 111

23 De div. qu. LXXXIII 46.2

24 De vera rel. xxxi 58; 254

25 Conf. XII xv 19; 280

26 ibid. For the relation of these ideas to those of Plotinus cf. A. H. Armstrong, 'Spiritual or intelligible Matter in Plotinus and St Augustine' in *Augustinus Magister* (Paris, 1954) 277f.; also A. H. Armstrong and R. A. Markus, *Christian Faith and Greek Philosophy* (London, 1960) 28f.

27 cf. P. Woollcott, 'Some Consideration of Creativity and
   Religious Experience in St Augustine of Hippo' in *Journal for
   the Scientific Study of Religion*, Spring 1966, 277
28 Conf. XII xiii 16; 278
29 Conf. XII vii 7; 274
30 De nat. boni xviii; 331; cf. Conf. XII vi 6 for the development
   of this concept in Augustine's mind.
31 De Gen. ad litt. V 23; Przywara, op. cit., 119
32 For the relation of Augustine's idea to those of Gregory of
   Nyssa cf. Ladner, op. cit. (Idea of Reform), 174f.
33 De Gen. ad litt. V 23; W. A. Christian in *A Companion to the
   Study of St Augustine*, ed. R. W. Battenhouse, 330
34 De Trin. III 16; Dods VII, 93–4
35 Gilson, op. cit., 207; cf. R. A. Markus, 'Marius Victorinus and
   Augustine' in *The Cambridge History of Greek and Early
   Medieval Philosophy*, ed. A. H. Armstrong (Cambridge, 1967)
   398–9. One must beware of pressing the picture Augustine
   developed for one reason to yield support for the view that he
   foresaw the idea of the development of one species into another
   in an evolutionary sense. He would have been more at home
   with the *Double Helix* than the *Origin of Species*.
36 cf. R. M. Grant, *Miracle and Natural Law* (Amsterdam, 1952)
   216f.
37 cf. Lyttkens, op. cit., 113
38 C.D. XII 2; 473
39 De lib. arb. II iii 7; 138
40 C.D. V 11; 196
41 De Trin. XV 3; 129–30
42 op. cit., 115
43 Tr. in Jo. Ev. XXIII 10; I 337; cf. John Burnaby's comment
   that when Augustine studied analogies for the Trinity all his
   'trinities' were psychological—LCC VIII 130 n9.
44 Carré, op. cit., 19; e.g. Conf. X xxxv 54; Enchir. iii 9
45 De Gen. ad litt. VII 24; Pope, op. cit., 208
46 Conf. X xxxv 57; 235
47 C.D. XXI 4; 968
48 De Gen. ad litt. I 19; cf. Carré, op. cit., 19
49 cf. Pope, op. cit., 207–25; H. I. Marrou, *Saint Augustin et la
   culture antique* (Paris, 1938) 135f.
50 A curiosity 'typical of the literary life of the Roman empire'.
   Grant, op. cit., 119
51 C. Faust. xxi 6; 266

52 cf. Conf. V iii 6
53 C.D. XII 4; 475
54 De Gen. ad litt. IX 17; C. N. Cochrane, *Christianity and Classical Culture* (Oxford, 1940) 441
55 op. cit., 441
56 De Trin. III 11; Dods VII, 88
57 cf. a similar view in Philo, H. A. Wolfson, *Philo* (Harvard, 1947) I 351
58 C.D. XXI 8; 980
59 C. Faust. xxvi 3; 321
60 Grant, op. cit., 217
61 E. N. Pickman, *The Mind of Latin Christendom* (Oxford, 1937) 212
62 *De Pulchro et Apto* has not survived.
63 cf. De Trin. VI 11–12; Dods VII, 177–8
64 De lib. arb. II xvi 41; 161
65 cf. Van Der Meer, op. cit., 320
66 ibid.
67 ibid.
68 Van Der Meer, op. cit., 324
69 En. in Ps. 41.7; II 184
70 cf. Van Der Meer, op. cit., 73
71 Conf. X vi 8; 205–6
72 De nat. boni i; 326
73 C.D. XI 22; 453
74 ibid.
75 C.D. XI 23
76 C.D. XI 22; 454
77 Conf. XIII xxxii 47; 329f.
78 Burnaby, op. cit., 148
79 C.D. XI 27; 460–1
80 De nat. boni iii; 327
81 ibid. iv
82 Ench. iv 12; 343; cf. Conf. III vii 12; Gilson, op. cit., 143f.; T. A. Lacey, *Nature, Miracle and Sin* (London, 1916) 93; Bonner, op. cit., 196f.
83 *Foolishness to the Greeks* (London, 1953) 45
84 Enneads I 8.3
85 op. cit., 201f.
86 cf. J. Hick, 'Evil' in *The Encyclopedia of Philosophy* 3 (London, 1967)
87 De incarn. 4; 29f.

88 J. S. Mackenzie, 'Notes on the Problem of Time' in *Mind*, 1912, 346—quoted by Dora Marsden, *The Philosophy of Time* (Oxford, 1955) 7

89 Conf. XI xiv 17; 254

90 cf. W. B. Green, 'St Augustine on Time' in *Scottish Journal of Theology*, June 1965, 148

91 C. Rau, 'Theories of Time in Ancient Philosophy' in *The Philosophical Review*, 62, 1953, 521

92 ibid.

93 R. Jordan, 'Time and Contingency in St Augustine' in *The Review of Metaphysics* 8, 1954–5, 395

94 Rau, op. cit., 524

95 cf. J. F. Callahan, *Four Views of Time in Ancient Philosophy* (Harvard, 1948)—further bibliography in Ladner, op. cit. (Idea of Reform), 203f.

96 op. cit., 162

97 cf. J. F. Callahan, in *Harvard Studies in Classical Philology* 63, 1958, 437f. A case is built for the dependence of Conf. XI xxiii 29 on Basil's *Adversus Eunomium* I 21. We know that Augustine had limited facility with the Greek language and that *Adversus Eunomium* had not been translated into Latin. If Augustine was dependent on Basil, he took 'kantharos' for a vase and thus changed Basil's picture of a beetle in motion to a potter's wheel. This is the sort of mistake he might make in assimilating a Greek author.

98 Conf. XI xii 14; 253

99 Conf. XI xiii 15; 253

100 Markus, op. cit. (Cambridge History), 403

101 Conf. XI xv 19; 255

102 Conf. XI xv 20; 256

103 Markus, op. cit. (Cambridge History), 404

104 Conf. XI xvi 21; 256

105 ibid.

106 Conf. XI xxvi 33; 263

107 cf. Conf. XI xxiii 29; 260

108 Conf. XI xxvi 33; 264

109 cf. R. Suter, 'Augustine on Time with some criticisms from Wittgenstein' in *Revue Internationale de Philosophie* 16, 1962, 385

110 Conf. XI xxviii 37; 266

111 ibid.

112 Conf. XI xxxi 41; 269. For further criticism of Augustine's view cf. Suter, op. cit., 386f. and Jordan, op. cit., 400f.

113 Strom. VII 70; 138

114 Strom. VI 100; ANCL XII 2, 361–2

115 Strom. II 140; ANCL XII 2, 79

116 Symposium IX 4; 138. cf. n36 in ACW XXVII, 233, on the obscurity in meaning of the reference in this passage to those who 'even though they are not committing fornication, are yet deluded into enjoying their sole and lawful spouses to *excess*'.

117 Strom. III 57–8; 66–7

118 H. Chadwick, *Alexandrian Christianity*, LCC II, 36

119 cf. Bonner, op. cit., 131

120 De serm. Dom. I xiv 39; 49

121 Ep. 262. 11; Loeb 239, 519

122 De bono conj. i 1; 275

123 De bono conj. viii 8; 283

124 De mor, eccl. xxx 63–4; 58

125 C.D. XIV 16; 577

126 C.D. XIV 24

127 Dorothea Krook, *Three Traditions of Moral Thought* (Cambridge, 1959) 274

128 ibid. 275

129 cf. D. S. Bailey, *The Man-Woman Relation in Christian Thought* (London, 1959)

130 He was not alone in failure at this point. What worried John Chrysostom most about sexual relations was the loss of self-control involved; the clouding of reason by bodily desire and passion. I owe this point to an unpublished thesis by Fr Peter Hocken.

131 cf. Pailin, op. cit.

132 cf. G. D. Yarnold, *The Moving Image* (London, 1966); B. H. Kellet, 'Time and Eternity' in *The Church Quarterly*, April 1971

CHAPTER FIVE

On *The City of God*

B Y A N Y standards the *City of God* is a remarkable book. It is a very long book : 1091 pages in the new Pelican translation; about a quarter of a million words in the Latin text. It was written over a considerable period—thirteen years from 413 to 426—and published in parts.[1] It is a diffuse piece of writing. Dom Gregory Dix called it a 'brilliant but uneven book'.[2] This is due undoubtedly to the distractions in the life of a busy bishop. But many of the digressions and tensions so characteristic of this work can be traced to the constant interplay in Augustine's mind of personal experience and strong rationality. This at once enriches the work and increases the difficulty in being sure that we have grasped all he is saying to us. Augustine was not the systematic thinker we would like him to be. The *City of God* is full of diversions and allusions to the writings of antiquity.[3] Some of the diversions provide the liveliest pages in the book. Augustine's curiosity about strange features of the natural world and his descriptions of contemporary miracles can hardly fail to fascinate.[4] J. N. Figgis lists some of the subjects taken into the book : 'the relation of true philosophy to scepticism, the idea of creation, the problem of time, the contribution of Platonism, more especially Neo-Platonism, the meaning of miracle and nature, the Incarnation as expressing the humility of God, the whole scheme of redemption, salvation by grace, long divagations into comparative mythology.'[5] Nevertheless it can properly be claimed that the *City of God* is 'Augustine's most carefully planned work'.[6] The first ten books are devoted to a destruction of pagan arguments against Christianity and the remainder to an exposition of the theme of the rise, growth and 'ends' of the two cities.[7]

Few books have had more influence on subsequent centuries than the *City of God*. The fact that Charlemagne liked to have it read to him is often mentioned.[8] Montaigne too was a great reader of the *City of God*.[9] However, few books with such influence have been so ill-understood. Augustine's political realism did not echo in the attitudes of medieval thinkers.[10] Theories were read out of him, or read into him, that were quite different from his own.[11] The political and social entity we call Christendom was claimed to be built on Augustinian foundations.[12] Sometimes, as with Pope Gregory I, he was understood,[13] but often he was not, and many of his important ideas were ignored or taken out of their context and used for polemical purposes.[14]

The character of the book

How, then, may the *City of God* be properly appreciated? It is not surprising that there is no easy answer to this. Altaner classes the work among Augustine's apologetic writings.[15] This view is taken by Baynes in his lecture on the political ideas in the *City of God*.[16] 'It is primarily concerned neither with politics nor social ideals. It is designed as a defence of the Christian religion; it is the last and the greatest of the Apologies for Christianity produced by the early Church.'[17] Others have seen it as a massive philosophy or theology of history. But it would be quite proper to see this as derivative from its essential apologetic character. Strictly speaking Augustine does not give us in the *City of God* a philosophy of history.[18] What we are offered is, among many other things, a theological interpretation of history. Reason could not perceive the action of God which Augustine describes under the figures of the two cities. The biblical imagery provides a clue and on the basis of this 'revelation' human history can be described in the form he gives.[19] I do not wish to deny these or any other approaches,[20] but I shall attempt to emphasize the pastoral nature of the whole enterprise.

Occasion for writing

The occasion that prompted the writing of the *City of God* was the fall of Rome before Alaric in 410. In the two previous years the city had been beseiged on two occasions.[21] The sack lasted, according to Orosius, for three days and was marked by the relative clemency of the invaders.[22] Alaric was an Arian Christian who gave orders that life should be spared and, in particular, the lives of those who sought refuge in the churches.[23] Rome did not

meet the major requirement of Alaric: a plentiful supply of corn.
So quickly he moved further south. He was not an invader from
outside the Empire bent on destruction, but one who sought to
secure a place for himself and his tribe within the Empire—
being supported by and living off it.[24] From an economic or
political point of view the fall of Rome was not disastrous. It
was no longer the capital of the Empire and the whole political
machine was independent of Rome. Far more serious was the
barbarian devastation of Gaul in 406.[25] Nevertheless the fall of
Rome served as a symbol through which could be expressed a
whole range of fears that had been building up in many people's
minds—unexpressed until this event justified their expression.

Only the innocent could be surprised by the fall of Rome. But,
like an anticipated bereavement, there came a sense of shock
when a familiar symbol of stability had been removed. Theo-
dosius II reacted quite sensibly to the example of Rome's vulner-
ability by building great walls round Constantinople to protect
the Eastern capital.[26] Some, like well-meaning but insensitive
sympathizers who refuse to talk with the bereaved about their
grief, kept silent about the whole episode. 'The Sack of Rome
was too uncomfortable a memory to be made the subject of
literature.'[27] A variety of people had their emotional investments
in Rome. It housed the temples symbolizing the old religions. It
was the shrine of Peter and Paul.[28] In a more general way it
served as a symbol of a secure framework within which life was
lived. So Pelagius, an observer of the fall itself, could say:
'Rome, the mistress of the world, shivered, crushed with fear, at
the sound of blaring trumpets and the howling of the Goths.'[29]
Jerome was more shrill in his hysteria: 'My voice sticks in my
throat; and, as I dictate, sobs choke my utterance. The City
which had taken the whole world was itself taken . . . "O God,
the heathen have come into thine inheritance".'[30] 'The bright
light of all the world was put out, or, rather, when the Roman
Empire was decapitated, and, to speak more correctly, the whole
world perished in one city.'[31] The feeling of despair and paralysis
that Jerome displayed, so like the bereaved, culminated in his
changing of the poet Lucan's words to: 'If Rome be lost, where
shall we look for help?' There is more here than the sadness of

an expatriate Roman. How had Rome become such a powerful symbol?

Early views of the Empire

For the early Church Christ had opened up new possibilities for mankind. The breaking down of the dividing wall between Jew and Gentile was seen as a foretaste of an organic unity of all men in Christ. Before this goal was achieved Christians had to live in a world recognizing distinctions between men and women, bond and free, Jews and Gentiles. There existed an Emperor who laid claim to taxes and temporal authorities to whom obedience was due out of divinely imposed duty.[32] Nevertheless the Christian had to keep his eye towards the future when God would bring his kingdom as the crown and culmination of history.[33] In the meantime he had to tolerate the tension between his hope and hard reality. It is not surprising that the pain of this was projected on to Rome, which became the symbol of what, as it were, stood between him and perfect felicity. This we find reflected in the imagery of the Revelation of John. Rome is : 'the great whore . . . drunk with the blood of God's people and with the blood of those who had borne testimony to Jesus.'[34] But this attitude was not the only one to be found in the period before Constantine. The four beasts of the Book of Daniel were seen to signify four universal monarchies through which history would run its course. The disintegration of the last of these empires would usher in the end of the world.[35] In the early Christian period the Greek empire had passed away and the end had not come, so it was assumed that the fourth monarchy was the Roman empire.[36] So, in the second century, Tertullian could say that Christians should 'pray for emperors, even for the whole state of the Empire and the fortunes of Rome, since we know that the great force which is threatening the whole world and the end itself of world-history which threatens terrible afflictions is being kept back by the respite granted to the Roman empire'.[37] The influence of apocalyptic writings had turned the end of the world into a threat not a blessing. Similarly Lactantius in the fourth century states : 'The fall and ruin of the world will shortly take place; except that while the city of Rome remains it appears that nothing of this kind is to be feared.'[38] Standing alongside this current of thinking was Origen with his idea that the unification of the Roman world had been part of God's providential design that enabled the Christian faith to be propagated.[39] 'God was preparing the nations for his teaching, that they might be under one Roman emperor, so that the unfriendly attitude of the nations to one another, caused by the existence of a large number of kingdoms, might not make it more difficult for Jesus' apostles to do what he commanded them when he said, "Go and teach all nations".'[40] This more favourable attitude to Rome was reinforced once the persecution of Christians ceased.

Response to Constantine

When Constantine granted toleration to the Church in 312 this 'volte-face on the State's part took the wind out of the sails of some widely current representations of the Empire'.[41] Now the possibility had emerged of the Church not standing over against Rome, but seeing the unity of the Empire bound up with the unity of the Faith. The great champion of this view was Eusebius. He was at Caesarea in a situation where Origen's influence was still felt and he certainly followed some of his theological ideas and exegetical methods. He took a similar positive attitude to Rome. This was consequent upon his view that the contrast between Christian society and human society in general was not fundamental. He saw history as an account of Christian triumph. Constantine had made it possible to look no longer in terms of inevitable conflict between Church and world, but rather the Christianization of the world.[42] Eusebius, like Origen, found the world ordered to receive the coming of Christ. The prophecy of Isaiah 2 : 4 was fulfilled. 'Immediately all the multitude of rulers among the Romans began to be abolished, when Augustus became sole ruler at the time of our Saviour's appearance.'[43] From this followed a partnership that benefited all men. 'As the knowledge of one God, and one way of religion and salvation, even the doctrine of Christ, was made known to all mankind; so at the self-same period, the entire dominion of the Roman empire being vested in a single sovereign, profound peace reigned throughout the world. And thus, by the express appointment of the same God, two roots of blessing, the Roman empire, and the doctrine of Christian piety, sprang up together for the benefit of men.'[44] This romantic view of early Christian history could be given more firmness when Constantine came into the picture. So Eusebius closes his *Ecclesiastical History* : 'Old ills were forgotten and oblivion cast on every deed of impiety; present good things were enjoyed, with the further hope of those which were yet to come...'[45] In all this, N. H. Baynes argues,[46] Eusebius was setting out a conception of the imperial government as a terrestrial copy of the rule of God in heaven and the Roman emperor as the Viceregent of the Christian God.[47] In poetical form this optimism was expressed by Prudentius : 'Shall we then doubt that Rome, dedicated to thee, O Christ, and placed under thy governance, with all her people and her foremost citizens, is now eagerly extending her earthly realm beyond the lofty stars of the great firmament.'[48] Those who had imbibed ideas of this sort could not fail to be shocked when the Goths entered Rome.

Augustine's response to Rome's fall

Augustine had to react to the fall of Rome on a number of fronts. He was too stable a man to react with hysterical despair. He was too honest to choose the alternative of a facile optimism that minimized the impact of the barbarian onslaught on the Empire.[49] He had to face those critics of Christianity who blamed the decline in Imperial power on the Christian ethic of turning the other cheek.[50] Also there were those who remembered the warning of Symmachus, when the Altar of Victory was removed from the Senate in Rome in 382, that the neglect of the gods would rebound upon the city.[51] It was important that he should meet these reactions and he attempted to do so. But chiefly he saw his responsibility not to answer the attacks of those outside as to administer consolation to Christians.[52] This he did by responding as a man, African bishop and theologian—trying to describe a way of looking at the world, firmly based on Christian doctrines, that enabled people to possess stability in an unstable world.

Augustine was, happily, a man who could afford to change his mind. It would be easier for students of his writings if this was not so, but it is in his freedom to rethink his position that his genius is expressed. R. A. Markus has carefully described the change in attitude that took place in his view of the Roman empire.[53]

'From the 390s for some ten or fifteen years, Augustine appears
to have joined the chorus of his contemporaries in their trium-
phant jubilation over the victory of Christianity.'[54] He could see
the 'kings of the earth now happily subdued by Christ, and all
nations serving him'.[55] Later he came to see the idea of a
Christian empire as a mirage.[56] Two years before the fall of
Rome Augustine recognized in a letter to Nectarius the conflict
of interests that can arise between the Christian and the citizen
of the empire: 'You must excuse us if, for the sake of that
country which we desire never to leave, we cause some
distress to that country which you desire to leave in the full
bloom of honour and prosperity.'[57] Augustine's mature position
may be described as follows: 'The Roman Empire has lost its
religious significance. Rome has been removed from the *Heilsgeschichte*, the Empire is no longer seen as God's chosen instrument for the salvation of men. It is no longer indispensable for
the unfolding of his providential plan in history.'[58] This was a
development of crucial significance. Augustine's rejection of the
Eusebian view made possible the development of a view in the
West that was subtly different from the Byzantine view of an
all-embracing Christian society. At times the likeness was very
close, but Western thinkers could not completely submit to
the attractions of the Eusebian view without falling over
Augustine.

Augustine's immediate reaction to the fall of Rome was,
typically, not just to answer the questions people were asking but
to probe behind them to more fundamental issues. When people
in his congregation questioned the providential care of a God
who could allow the devastation of Rome, in spite of the presence
there of the tombs of Peter and Paul, Augustine drew their attention to Job who, similarly facing disaster, had worked through
it to discern it as a testing of the nature of his faith.[60] Unlike
Sodom, Rome was not completely destroyed; its affliction was
a chastisement.[61] What he wanted to do was wean his people
away from putting their faith in inadequate symbols of security.
'Let us not then faint, my brethren: an end there will be to all
earthly kingdoms.'[62] God takes away false security to enable men
to see their inadequacy. 'Those ... who follow and long after
earthly things, who place their hope in earthly things, when these

they have lost, whether they will or no, what shall they retain? were shall they abide? Nothing without, nothing within.'[63]

To the accusation that the fall of Rome was consequent upon the adoption of Christianity within the empire, Augustine gives his attention in a correspondence with Marcelinus in the year 412. Volusianus, in conversation, had raised with Marcellinus the argument that to turn the other cheek was inconsistent with the duty of the good citizen[64] and that 'it is manifest that very great calamities have befallen the commonwealth under the government of emperors observing, for the most part, the Christian religion'.[65] To this Augustine replied with a typically subtle exposition of Matthew 5:39 in which he suggested that the text could not have been intended to be taken literally because the left, not the right cheek is likely to be first hit by a right-handed assailant.[66] He went on to claim that the text teaches that 'temporal things ought to be despised in comparison with eternal things, as the left is in comparison with the right'.[67] Augustine faced the more important issue by claiming that the pagans praised the virtues that were now being blamed as Christian innovations,[68] and that the empire was decaying from within long before the coming of Christ.[69]

We must remember also that Augustine was an African. He had indeed absorbed much of the Latin spirit, but his roots were in Africa. It is not surprising, then, that at the fall of Rome he was on the side of African apologists who maintained that the city's rise was due to injustice.[70] At a notorious stage in the Donatist controversy he had to appeal to the secular powers, but this is in conflict with a general independence that was a mark of the African spirit.[71] But above all Augustine was a bishop and a theologian. As Burleigh puts it: 'He had responsibilities unknown to the monk at Bethlehem. If the world falls in ruins, a bishop must stand by his people to comfort and strengthen them.'[72] Augustine's heart, unlike that of Jerome, was not broken by the fall of Rome. He had more personal problems near at hand. A converted Donatist had lapsed through being cold-shouldered by the Catholics. 'At that news, I tell you, brethren, my heart was broken.'[73] He must enable his people to learn fundamental things from what was happening around them. 'As men betake themselves in greater haste to a place of greater

security when they see in the shaking of their walls the ruin of
the house impending, so ought Christians, the more that they
perceive, from the increasing frequency of their afflictions, that
the destruction of this world is at hand, to be more prompt and
active in transferring to the treasury of heaven the good which
they were proposing to store up on earth.'[74] Augustine was by
this time an old man and had passed through the stage of life
that Jung describes in which it is hygienic 'to discover in death
a goal towards which one can strive'.[75] Out of this experience he
could declare: 'The world is perishing, the world is waxing old,
the world is failing; is distressed by the heavy breathing of old
age. But do not fear. Thy youth shall be renewed as the eagle's.'[76]
This renewal would come, not as they received personal affir-
mation by their membership of a stable civilization, but from
their membership of a 'city with firm foundations, whose archi-
tect and builder is God'.[77]

The conflict of sin and grace

Writing the *Confessions* was an act of praise and thanksgiving
for the good and bad in Augustine's personal history. Having
told his own history in books I–IX Augustine looked at the way
in which man searches for God and then considered creation as
the setting for each man's personal history. In book XI he
expresses the desire to speak of the wonder of God seen 'from the
very beginning, when thou madest heaven and earth, and thence-
forward to the everlasting reign of thy Holy City with thee'.[78]
This desire is fulfilled in the *City of God*. But it was not to be a
chronicle. All the experience of Augustine as a man who had
known the conflict of sin and grace within himself was to shape
the work. So O'Meara sees the *City of God* as an application to
the whole history of mankind of the sort of analysis he made of
himself in *Confessions*;[79] or, as J. N. Figgis put it: 'Much of the
book is but an expansion of Augustine's doctrine of grace applied
on the scale of world history.'[80] As Augustine had in the *Confessions* to take the measure of his past, so in the *City of God*
he had to explore the whole culture into which he had been born,
and from which he drew so deeply, and submit it to valuation
in the light of Christ.[81]

The source of the image

Augustine had one model with which to work: the idea of the pilgrim people led, from Abraham onwards, towards the promised land—a way that, he claims, surpasses Porphyry's 'universal way of liberation for the soul'.[82] He also paralleled the seven ages of man by a description of the totality of human history in the seven ages of the world.[83] This provides the frame within which the reformation of man takes place.[84] When Augustine speaks of 'the origin, development and appointed end' of the two cities[85] it is human history seen as a development that occurs between the beginning and the end. His use of the word 'procursus' does not imply 'progress' or 'development' in the modern sense. It is a neutral term—the lines along which the interaction between man and God proceeds.[86] Whatever order is given to this process is not externally imposed. In one sense God is not pushing events along in a predetermined way. What order it is possible to discern in the history of mankind derives from the impulse of human beings to attain happiness. The ways they choose to find happiness are determined by their desires. The fact that these desires fall into either *amor sui* or *amor Dei* provides the clue for making an orderly description of human history. The image that Augustine used to make this description was two cities.

Augustine states that the source of the image he uses is the Bible. 'The City of God of which we are treating is vouched for by those Scriptures whose supremacy over every product of human genius does not depend on the chance impulses of the minds of men, but is manifestly due to the guiding power of God's supreme providence, and exercises sovereign authority over the literature of all mankind. Now in this Scripture we find these words, "Glorious things have been said of you, City of God".'[87] Many passages he quotes, or alludes to, give him this source.[88] With his great knowledge of classical culture and Christian literature to draw upon there was much that linked with this idea. Some of this has been absorbed into the way he used the image and some is rejected. Ambrose had commented on the contrast between the City of God and the Kingdom of the world.[89] Modern study has put particular emphasis upon the influence of the Donatist lay expositor of the Bible: Tyconius.

There is no doubt that Augustine had a high regard for him. He commended and used his 'rules' for the exposition of Scripture.[90] From the quotations in Beatus of Liebana it has been possible to reconstruct Tyconius's commentary on the Apocalypse. This shows a number of points of similarity with Augustine. Tyconius and Augustine use similar language; they distinguish the invisible church from the institution; they both see the Catholic and Donatist churches as mixed bodies of saints and sinners.[91] But we are not justified in seeing Tyconius as the direct source of Augustine's ideas—both saw themselves as expositors of a common source : the Bible. It is not the case that Augustine created a philosophy of history 'by taking Plato's *Republic* and Christianizing it into his *City of God*'.[92] There are resemblances, but Plato's interest, and that of Cicero building on his model, was primarily political. Augustine had drawn his Platonism chiefly from Plotinus, in whom there was an abandonment of political interest.[93] In any case, in his mature writing, the Platonist in Augustine was always subordinate to his responsibility as a Biblical expositor. In a similar way, it may be that Virgil's *Aeneid* can be discerned as a typological reference throughout the City of God.[94] The likeness of Virgil's account of the origin and growth of the Roman empire—a sort of pilgrimage to the promised land—may have lurked in the back of Augustine's mind,[95] but at the forefront was biblical history. If we are to view rightly the City of God we must see it not as an incursion into Christianity of a somewhat alien classical world, but primarily as a biblical image freshly conceived to which all classical associations are subservient.

Augustine did not arrive at the imagery he uses in the *City of God* when he sat down to write the work. Twenty years before the fall of Rome he had written : 'The entire human race, whose life, like the life of an individual from Adam to the end of the world, is so arranged by the laws of divine providence that it appears divided among two classes. In one of these is the multitude of the impious who bear the image of the earthly man from the beginning to the end of the world. In another is the succession of the people devoted to the one God.'[96] And in 400 this classification is represented in terms of two cities : 'Two cities, one of the wicked, the other of the Saints, are carried down from the beginning of the human race even to the end of the world; now united in their bodies, but separated in their wills, but in the day of Judgement destined to be separated in their bodies also.'[97] Not surprisingly, in the light of the subject for exposition many references can be found in the sermons on the Psalms. There is 'Babylon wherein we are captives, and Jerusalem for a return to which we are sighing. For these two cities, according to the letter, in reality are two cities. . . . Two loves make up these two cities : love of God maketh Jerusalem, love of the world maketh Babylon.'[98] All this previous thinking was combined with earlier images reaching right back to Cassiciacum, with his description of two men on a journey[99], when Augustine came to write the *City of God*, which he describes as *magnum opus et arduum.*[100]

The nature of the two cities

In the ancient world the household gods created the solidarity of the family. More important than ties of birth or affection were the religious symbols. Social groups larger than the family were created, as gods common to more than one family developed.[101] Thus one can see the city as that grouping of people who were united by common religion.[102] Augustine saw human groupings as being dependent upon things held in common. So he could define a city generally as 'simply a united multitude of individuals'[103] or accept Cicero's definition : 'an association united by a common sense of right and a community of interest' and in particular his requirement of justice.[104] It is notoriously difficult to define community,[105] and though Augustine is aware of the problem when he comes to describe *civitas Dei* and *civitas terrena*, it is clear that he is using these terms as images rather than defined entities. 'I classify the human race into two branches : the one consists of those who live by human standards, the other of those who live according to God's will. I also call these two classes the two cities, *speaking allegorically.*'[106] There are two special features of his conception which make clear that he is describing history in theological terms. One is the special nature of the bond that creates the community. 'The two cities were created by two kinds of love : the earthly city was created by self-love reaching the point of contempt for God, the

Heavenly City by the love of God carried as far as contempt of self.'[107] The second is the eschatological framework within which he works. 'By two cities I mean two societies of human beings, one of which is predestined to reign with God for all eternity, the other doomed to undergo eternal punishment with the Devil.'[108] The first of these enabled Augustine to look beneath the surface of the flow of human history and set out a scheme that intertwined, but rarely coincided with, a historian's view. The second freed him from the pressure of the immediate events that formed the background to his writing. The fall of Rome was one small item in human affairs and could only be valued correctly in the light of the final outcome of the human story. He contrasted the Christian martyrs and the Roman heroes who 'belonged to an earthly city, and the aim set before them, in all their acts of duty for her, was the safety of their country, and a kingdom not in heaven, but on earth; not in life eternal, but in the process where the dying pass away and are succeeded by those who will die in their turn'.[109]

The use of the image
Using these images Augustine was able to comprehend the whole of human history. Every man and his contribution to the historical process could be located in one city or the other according to the direction of his desires. Those who are turned towards God belong to a solidarity that runs from the beginning to the end of time. At any particular time it is not possible to distinguish in any absolute way between those who are and those who are not of the City of God. 'Both cities alike enjoy the good things, or are afflicted with the adversities of this temporal state, but with a different faith, a different expectation, a different love, until they are separated by the final judgement, and each receives her own end, of which there is no end.'[110] In this view he follows his earlier thought[111] and that of Cyprian, who was the first to apply the parable of the wheat and tares to the situation of the Church.[112] So on one level history can be regarded in a purely secular manner. Even the institutional boundaries of the Church do not provide the evidence to permit a *heilsgeschichte*. But on another level, hidden within the historical process, there exist these two solidarities of men. Their existence is perceived by the

eye of faith, but their actual composition will only be known at
the end of history.

On the basis of the image of the two cities, with the limitations
that he built into it, Augustine used book after book to comment
upon the history of man in this world. In the biblical material
he reviewed, he believed that revelation had shown into which
city certain men and their affairs could be designated. 'Cain was
the first son born to those two parents of mankind, and he belonged to the city of man; the later son, Abel, belonged to the
City of God. . . . Scripture tells us that Cain founded a city,
whereas Abel, as a pilgrim, did not found one. For the City of
the saints is up above, although it produces citizens here below,
and in their persons the City is on pilgrimage until the time of its
kingdom comes.'[113] Similarly he saw the city of the world expressed in the tower of Babel (or Babylon) story[114] because 'the
name "Babylon" means, in fact, "confusion" '[115] and can thus
be contrasted with the City of God which has the quality of
'peace'. 'There will be true peace, where none will suffer attack
from within himself nor from any foe outside.'[116] When Augustine
looked at history outside the biblical revelation he had only the
criteria attached to his image to guide him. His treatment of
this material is in the form of examples of the way *amor sui*
expresses itself in human affairs. So, though he does not consign
Rome to the city of this world in any final sense, its character
and practices are compared with the ideal City of God and its
people exhorted 'to add themselves to the number of its
citizens'.[117]

As a pastor to his people the Bishop, Augustine, had to use
the occasion of the fall of Rome to make the point he had made
in so many ways, on so many occasions, that Christians must get
their values and affections rightly ordered. In so far as they had
failed in this, they had to accept suffering as a chastisement for
their sins. So he condemned those Christians who, by attending
the theatres, displayed their unwillingness to learn the lesson of
chastisement. There were those who 'do not hesitate to murmur
against God, whose sacramental sign they bear, even in the
company of his acknowledged enemies. At one time they join his
enemies in filling the theatres, at another they join with us in
filling the churches'.[118] The Christian is set within a neutral

secular world. God has willed that 'temporal goods and temporal evils should befall good and bad alike, so that the good things should not be too eagerly coveted, when it is seen that the wicked also enjoy them, and that the evils should not be discreditably shunned, when it is apparent that the good are often afflicted with them'.[119] What matters is the response the Christian makes —in what direction his affection moves. So Paulinus of Nola is set up as an example, for he 'deliberately reduced himself from great wealth to extreme poverty and the great riches of holiness; and when the barbarians devastated Nola, and he was in their hands, he prayed in his heart, as I learnt from him afterwards, "Lord, let me not be tortured on account of gold and silver; for you know where all my riches are" '.[120]

Relationship to theological themes

Apart from the *City of God's* apologetic purpose, is it just a massive piece of preaching? In one sense it is. But it is a subtle drawing together of the major doctrinal themes that set out the Christian's relationship to the world. Anders Nygren described as the three fundamental dogmas of the early Church: creation, incarnation and resurrection.[121] Through these doctrines Christians expressed their stance towards the world. In confessing God as creator they rejected the view that it is from the material world that men need to be saved. Incarnation was a declaration that God met man in his world. In resurrection, and particularly resurrection of the flesh, they stated that by God's grace existence is not tragic but is essentially a comedy that finds its fulfilment in God. These three strands come together and are blended in *Missale Romanum* of 1570 at the mixing of the water and wine: 'O God who in creating man didst exalt his nature very wonderfully and yet more wonderfully didst establish it anew, by the mystery signified in the mingling of this water and wine, grant us to have part in the Godhead of Him who hath vouchsafed to share our manhood, Jesus Christ, thy Son, our Lord.' In another form the synthesis is achieved in the *City of God*. Here also it is the Incarnation that unites man's life with his world and sets it firmly in the purposes of God. In Christ the Word assumed flesh and stretched out 'a hand to those who lay fallen'.[122] By doing so the 'true Mediator has shown that it is sin which is evil, not the substance or nature of flesh, since that substance could be assumed, with a human soul, and preserved free from sin, and could be laid aside in death, and changed into something better by resurrection'.[123] Christ had provided the means of throwing light upon the hidden purpose of history. Man can live in this world with his affections rightly directed so that he is not corrupted by this world but uses it properly.[124] At one level he cannot be distinguished from other secular men, but, as with Christ, hidden within him there is another element by which he is linked to God. Like the City of God as a whole, the individual citizen 'exists in this world of time, a stranger among the ungodly, living by faith' and also eschatologically 'in the security of (his) everlasting seat'.[125] The City of God has a continuous existence through history. It exists here in this world and, as it were, will flow through into eternity. There is no discontinuity at the boundary of this world and the next, only an extension of felicity. Childhood is not just a preparation for adult life; it is life itself. To learn what it means to be a child of God as a child is essentially the same as being a child of God in maturity.[126] So those who belong to the City of God may be its true citizens in this world and enjoy its greater richness when all history is gathered up. Augustine struggled for words in which to express this. He was caught up by the categories of his time and spoke of man as soul and flesh, but saw him as one whole. The terms ' "animal" and "carnal", are examples of the "part for whole" figure of speech. For *anima* (soul) and *caro* (flesh) are parts of a man, and can stand for man in his entirety'.[127] In resurrection 'the spiritual flesh will thus be subject to the spirit, but it will be flesh, not spirit, just as the carnal spirit was subject to the flesh, and yet was spirit, not flesh'.[128] In the end he had to be content with the power of his images rather than his words and ends his work with the conviction that the Christian moves towards that place where 'we shall be still and see; we shall see and we shall love; we shall love and we shall praise'. Such a fulfilment, and none other for Augustine, can define the purpose of life.

This view of the life of man shaped by the incarnational model —secular man with a hidden dimension—either proleptically in the case of those before Christ or created by grace in those who follow him—does not answer many of the prosaic questions we want to ask. We have to work with visible solidarities, like Church and State. We are faced by a whole range of ethical problems that demand solutions. Can we in some way construct a third city to take care of that which we cannot see as being part of the City of God and yet are unable to regard as destined for damnation? Will Augustine give some credence to our liberal thoughts? In one sense a definitely negative answer must be given.[129] The whole of human activity is essentially ambiguous. But this ambiguity prevents us from coming to any firm conclusions as to where, and where not, the activity of God is present in developing the City of God. Thus we can have, from an Augustinian point of view, sympathy with Karl Rahner's view of the 'Anonymous Christian'.[130] We can be churchmen, but from Augustine's viewpoint, we cannot sacralize the Church. We can take our place in the life of the State,[131] but we must always preserve our freedom to prophesy against it. Similarly in ethical questions we cannot determine good and bad—these will only be known in the last judgement—we have to deal with the taxing question of right and wrong, within the ambiguity of complex situations.[132]

Augustine was not prepared to replace the lost security of Rome and all it symbolized with other institutions or symbols that were no more secure. He could call men to faith—faith in Christ—that in him God had decisively associated himself with human life and that in Christ's resurrection and ascension they had been given a declaration of the power of God to lead history on beyond death into 'a comprehensive re-novation of the whole creation'.[133]

For a time of crisis

I first began to read the *City of God* in the 1950s when hydrogen-bombs were being tested. These were the days when civilization seemed to be under real threat. At that time the age of Augustine did not seem far away. A similar connection was made by E. H. Brookes in a book which related the *City of God* to the South African situation.[134] He likened Augustine to the one who answered Alfred in Chesterton's *Ballad of the White Horse* saying: 'I bring you naught for your comfort'. As we have said, Augustine did not offer, in the crisis of his time, comfort in the modern sense. He did not offer an alternative security system to the one his contemporaries had lost. What he did do was expose the inadequacy of the institutional forms of support we create, and offer the only true security available to men—an eschatological hope that enabled them to live, as someone has said, in a room without a floor.

It is just not true, as some have claimed,[135] that Augustine was not interested in life in this world. We have provided ample evidence that he grew completely out of his Manichaean period and he adapted his Neoplatonism to the demands of the Incarnation. He would have endorsed the view of Barth: 'When we have discovered man as God's creature at this point, in Jesus Christ, we have made direct discovery of heaven and earth as the object of the divine act of creation'.[136] This discovery prevents the Christian from denying his responsibility towards this world. Christian faith persuades men to 'benevolence, justice, and concord among themselves, as well as true piety towards God',[137] but it also requires them to remain critics of the institutional forms that seek to serve these objectives.[138] 'The fullest endorsement of secular value is tinged with criticism.'[139] The optimistic beliefs of the nineteenth century now seem to be so like those of Eusebius. We need the 'pessimistic realism'[140] of Augustine when we work within, for instance, community development programmes. Augustine cannot be used to support a refusal to engage in such activities. He can be used to give us more exacting standards by which to assess them. The same can be said of all other situations in which the Christian acts. As Moltmann has put it: 'Faith can have nothing to do with fleeing the world, with resignation and with escapism ... it espouses in all meekness the cause of the devastated earth and of harassed humanity' but 'peace with God means conflict with the world, for the goad of the promised future stabs inexorably into the flesh of every unfulfilled present'.[141] Augustine would keep us awake to the 'unfulfilled' in even the best of human activities. In this way Christians become in Harvey Cox's phrase, 'God's avant-garde'.[142] They do not seek to be 'at home' in any part of the social order but accept a more ambiguous relation with the world through which a word of prophecy can be heard.[143]

The Church itself is also involved in the ambiguity of life in this world. It contains members of both cities. 'It is from the Church that the reapers are to collect the tares which the Lord allowed to grow together with the wheat until the harvest.'[144] Nevertheless, just as, for practical purposes, Augustine tended to identify the Roman state with the *civitas terrena*, so he tends to regard the Church as synonymous with the *civitas Dei*. The subtle difference is described by Markus : 'Whereas with Rome the question was : given the dichotomy of the "two cities", where does Rome fit into the scheme? with the Church the question was rather : given the identity of the Church and the "heavenly city", where is the "earthly city" to be found within the Church?'[145] One may start with a basic loyalty to the Church as the sacramental community and the company of those who share in and support one's pilgrimage. But the Church is on pilgrimage and cannot be allowed to be so institutionalized that it provides a place of security. Augustine's opposition to Donatism was based on many grounds, but in many ways Donatism did represent an attempt to freeze the Church in one style of life. It stood for no compromise with the spirit of the age and anticipated a constant minority status for the Church.[146] Without the more obvious theological and sociological pressures to resist the movement, from the point of view of the *City of God* Augustine would have opposed it. He could retain the 'unholy' within the institutional Church without destroying the integrity of the City of God—the true unity of the Church being eschatological rather than empirical.[147] It is the objective of the Church that is to determine her life and not the pressure of passing forms that may be created from other sources. Without knowing it the angry young churchmen of the 1960s were Augustinian in their attitude and had a larger loyalty than many who supported the *status quo*. In fact more probably they were influenced by F. D. Maurice and his view of the corrupting power of 'systems' and of the Church as 'witness to the only true foundation of State, nations, families, and all human order'.[148]

Guided by Augustine's views, man can live in a pluralistic world because of the conviction that in the end all will be one, held in the unity of God. The future calls us because we have faith in 'the God who makes the dead live and summons things that are not yet in existence as if they already were'.[149] The future is not retarded by God's neglect, but our blind and obstinate resistance[150]—the resistance of those who have set their affections in an improper place. We struggle for the unity of all men properly only when we see them as having a common source and a single Father. However much we may hold this with our minds, Augustine comes to remind us that what truly matters is what we love. In learning through Christ to love God, and thus ourselves, our neighbour and our world, we contribute most to the fulfilment of God's purpose.

NOTES

1 cf. 'Note on the composition of the *De Civitate Dei*' by A. F. West in S. Angus, *The Sources of the First Ten Books of Augustine's De Civitate Dei* (Princeton, 1906)

2 *The Shape of the Liturgy* (London, 1945) 386 n1

3 cf. S. Angus, op. cit., Pt. I; J. O'Meara, *Charter of Christendom: The Significance of the City of God* (New York, 1961) 94

4 cf. D. Knowles (ed.), *Augustine: City of God* (Harmondsworth, 1972) xxx

5 op. cit.,3

6 Markus, op. cit. (Saeculum), 47

7 cf. the scheme set out in R. H. Barrow, *An Introduction to St Augustine's The City of God* (London, 1950) 18, based on Retr. II xliii.

8 cf. E. R. Hardy in *A Companion to the Study of St Augustine*, ed. Battenhouse, 257

9 Marrou, op. cit. (Influence), 170

10 cf. H. A. Deane, *The Political and Social Ideas of St Augustine* (New York, 1966) 229

11 cf. N. H. Baynes, 'The Political Ideas of St Augustine's De Civitate Dei' in *Byzantine Studies and Other Essays* (London, 1955) 304

12 cf. Cochrane, op. cit., 377

13 cf. F. E. Cranz, 'De Civitate Dei XV 2, and Augustine's Idea of the Christian Society' in *Speculum* XXV, April 1950, 221

14 cf. Deane, op. cit., 230f.

15 cf. Altaner, op. cit., 503

16 op. cit., 288

17 ibid.; similarly Figgis, op. cit., 29 and 36

18 cf. E. Gilson, 'Foreword' in *St Augustine The City of God*, ed. V. J. Bourke (New York, 1958) 22 n18

19 cf. Gilson, op. cit. (Foreword), 30

20 cf. TeSelle, op. cit., 269

21 Brown, op. cit. (Augustine), 288

22 cf. O'Meara, op. cit. (Charter), 4

23 cf. Barrow, op. cit., 19

24 cf. J. H. S. Burleigh, *The City of God. A Study of St Augustine's Philosophy* (London, 1949) 14

25 cf. Burleigh, op. cit., 15

26 cf. P. Brown, *The World of Late Antiquity* (London, 1971) 137

27 Burleigh, op. cit., 16

28 cf. Brown, op. cit. (Augustine), 289

29 Ep. ad Demetriadem 30; quoted in Brown, ibid.

30 Ep. 127 12; NPNF VI 257

31 Preface to Commentary on Ezekiel; 500

32 Eph. 2:11f.; Romans 13:1f.

33 cf. C. Dawson in *A Monument to St Augustine* (London, 1945) 45f.

34 Rev. 17:1 and 6

35 cf. T. E. Mommsen, 'St Augustine and the Christian Idea of Progress' in *Journal of the History of Ideas* XII, June 1951, 348

36 cf. H. H. Rowley, *Darius the Mede and the Four World Empires in the Book of Daniel* (Cardiff, 1959) 73f.

37 Apology 32; 99

38 Div. Inst. 7 25; 481. In the *Epitome* Lactantius did not seem to fear this event: chapter 72; E. H. Blakeney, *Lactantius' Epitome of the Divine Institutes* (London, 1950) 122–3. See also Blakeney's note on pp. 167–8.

39 cf. Markus, op. cit. (Saeculum), 48

40 C. Cels. II 30; 92

41 R. A. Markus, 'The Roman Empire in Early Christian Historiography' in *The Downside Review*, October 1963, 342

42 cf. Cranz, op. cit., 220–1

43 Praep. Ev. 1.4; 10

44 Laus Const. 16.4; 606

45 Eccles. Hist. 10.9.8; I 324

46 'Eusebius and the Christian Empire' in *Byzantine Studies and Other Essays* (London, 1955) 168f.

47 Baynes finds a number of models of Hellenistic Kingship that may be sources for Eusebius' view.

48 C. Symmachum i 587–90; quoted in Markus, op. cit. (Historiography), 345; cf. Markus, op. cit. (Saeculum), 27f. For other reactions to the collapse of the Empire see R. P. C. Hanson, 'The Reaction of the Church to the Collapse of the Western Roman Empire in the Fifth Century' in *Vigiliae Christianae* 26, December 1972, 272f.

49 cf. Markus, op. cit. (Cambridge History), 410

50 cf. Ep. 136.2; I 175

51 cf. TeSelle, op. cit., 268

52 cf. C.D. I 16; 26

53 op. cit. (Saeculum), 31f.

54 ibid.

55 C. Faust. xiii 7; 202

56 cf. Markus, op. cit. (Saeculum), 38

57 Ep. 91.2; I 383; Augustine is contrasting the eternal world with the world Nectarius must shortly leave by death.

58 Markus, op. cit. (Saeculum), 54–5

59 cf. Cranz, op. cit., 221

60 De urbis excidio 3f.

61 ibid.

62 Serm. 105. 11; I 428

63 ibid. 13; 431

64 Ep. 136.2; II 175

65 ibid.

66 Ep. 138.12; II 203; cf. Origen, De Princ. IV 3.3; 292

67 ibid.

68 cf. quotation from Juvenal in Ep. 138.16; II 207

69 cf. Augustine's quotation of Sallust : 'O venal city, and doomed to perish speedily, if only it could find a purchaser !' Ep. 138.16; II 207.

70 cf. W. H. C. Frend, *The Donatist Church* (Oxford, 1952) 231

71 cf. Dawson, op. cit., 53f.

72 op. cit., 17

73 Serm. 296.12; quoted Brown, op. cit. (Augustine), 290

74 Ep. 122.2; II 122

75 C. G. Jung, *Modern Man in Search of a Soul* (London, 1961) 129

76 Serm. 81.8; I 252–3

77 Heb. 11 :10

78 Conf. XI ii 3; 246

79 op. cit. (Charter), 16

80 op. cit., 6

81 cf. F. E. Cranz, 'The Development of Augustine's Ideas on Society before the Donatist Controversy' in *Harvard Theological Review* XLVII, October 1954, 287f.

82 C.D. X 32; 420f.

83 cf. De cat. rud. xxii 39; 228f.

84 cf. Ladner, op. cit. (Reformation), 876

85 C.D. I 35; 46

86 cf. Mommsen, op. cit., 371f.; Markus, op. cit. (Saeculum), 9f.

87 C.D. XI 1; 429

88 e.g. Ps 87:3, 48:2, 46:4; Heb. 11:10, 11:16, 12:22, 13:14; Rev. 3:12, 21:2

89 cf. Burleigh, op. cit., 103–4

90 cf. De doct. chr. III xxx 42; 104

91 cf. Barrow, op. cit., 271–2

92 W. Jaeger, *Paideia. The Ideals of Greek Culture* (Oxford, 1947) II 77

93 cf. Burleigh, op. cit., 157–8

94 cf. O'Meara, op. cit. (Augustine the Artist), 258

95 for certainly he was familiar with it—cf. Conf. I xiii 20; 42, also C. Acad. II iv 10; 74.

96 De vera rel. xxvii 50; 250

97 De cat. rud. xix 31; 221–2

98 En. in Ps. 64. 1–3; III 250–2. A detailed account of the development of Augustine's theme is found in A. Lauras and H. Rondet, 'Le Thème des Deux Citiés dans l'oeuvre de Saint Augustin' in *Études Augustiniennes* (Paris, 1953) 99f.

99 C. Acad. III xv 34; 138–9

100 C.D. I praefatio

101 cf. Gilson, op. cit. (Foreword), 15

102 cf. Barrow, op. cit., 267f.

103 C.D. I 13; 25

104 C.D. II 21; 73

105 One modern study listed 94 definitions; cf. C. Bell and H. Newby, *Community Studies* (London, 1971) 27

106 C.D. XV 1; 595

107 C.D. XIV 28; 593

108 C.D. XV 1; 595

109 C.D. V 14; 204

110 C.D. XVIII 54; 842

111 De cat. rud. xix 31; 221

112 Cyprian, Ep. 54.2; 116; cf. G. G. Willis, *St Augustine and the Donatist Controversy* (London, 1950) 121

113 C.D. XV 1; 596
114 Gen. 11 :1–10
115 C.D. XVI 4; 657
116 C.D. XXI 30; 1088
117 C.D. II 29; 86
118 C.D. I 35; 46
119 C.D. I 8; 13
120 C.D. I 10; 19
121 op. cit., 276
122 C.D. X 24; 405
123 ibid.
124 C.D. XIX 17
125 C.D. I praefatio; 5
126 cf. K. Rahner, Theological Investigations VIII, 33f.
127. C.D. XIV 4; 553
128 C.D. XXII 21; 1064
129 cf. H. I. Marrou, 'Civitas Dei, civitas terrena : num tertium quid?' in Studia Patristica II, 1957, 340f.
130 Theological Investigations VI, 390f. and VIII, 112f.
131 cf. Deane, op. cit. On the complex issue of Augustine's appeal to the state to endorse religious coercion during the Donatist controversy see Brown, op. cit. (Religion and Society), 260f.; Markus, op. cit. (Saeculum), 134f.; Willis, op. cit., 127f.
132 cf. L. Hodgson, 'Christian Citizenship. Some reflections on St Augustine, Ep. 138' in Church Quarterly Review, Oct.–Dec. 1947, 2
133 G. Florovsky, 'Echatology in the Patristic Age' in Studia Patristica II, 1957, 239
134 The City of God and the Politics of Crisis (Oxford, 1960)
135 e.g. F. Copleston, A History of Philosophy (London, 1946) II 74
136 op. cit. III. 1, 28
137 Ep. 138.17; II 208
138 cf. Hodgson, op. cit., 10
139 Markus, op. cit. (Saeculum), 168
140 Deane, op. cit., 241
141 J. Moltmann, Theology of Hope (London, 1967) 21
142 The Secular City (London, 1965) 125f.
143 cf. Markus, op. cit. (Saeculum), 165–6
144 C.D. XX 9; 914
145 op. cit. (Saeculum), 118
146 cf. TeSelle, op. cit., 273

147 cf. M. Wiles, *The Making of Christian Doctrine* (Cambridge, 1967) 149

148 A. R. Vidler, *The Theology of F. D. Maurice* (London, 1948) 67

149 Romans 4 : 17

150 cf. Cochrane, op. cit., 516

Epilogue

T H E search for relevance in theological studies is highly laudable. Theology must relate to life and be an expression of a dimension in life that is of great significance. But there is danger in an intense obsession with relevance, as there is in the person who is so intensely serious that he cannot afford the time to tell a joke. Sometimes we ought to be frank and admit that we read the writings of some men simply because they fascinate us—they reveal interesting people who are worth taking time to get to know. This is true for me as far as Augustine is concerned. I find him a fascinating person. When I begin to think I have understood him, I come across something that opens out a new line of exploration. Many-layered people of this sort are comparatively rare. It is human interest that makes one element of motivation for studying him. The fact that he is also a theologian of some complexity provides another. There is much in his theology that is illuminating. The fecundity of his mind provides many models that are exciting to work with. Augustine provides an example of the sort of theologian Lonergan calls for who, through self-knowledge, self-appropriation and self-possession, is able to provide a ground base from which conversation between many disciplines can proceed.[1] And yet I cannot find his theology wholly satisfying. I too feel the pressure of relevance. Many details of Augustine's thought can be argued over, and will be endlessly, but when I seek the centre of my dissatisfaction I find it in the Neoplatonic metaphysical assumptions that form the framework to all his thinking.

Too much can be made of Augustine's debt to Neoplatonism. Historical theologians always seem more willing to recognize the Hellenization of Christianity than the Christianization of Hellenism. Augustine wanted not only to clothe Christian thought with the grace of form that was Hellenism, but also to devote the whole apparatus of pagan culture to a Christian purpose. He took the command to the Israelites to 'plunder Egypt' before

they left it as justification for this programme. Christians are to
dig gold and silver 'from certain mines of divine Providence,
which is everywhere infused'.[2] The current categories of thought
available to him were those of Neoplatonism. At an early stage
these influenced him deeply.[3] Later, when he held a teaching
office within the Church, Augustine felt he had to interpret the
biblical revelation in the terms of his age. What is sauce for the
Bultmannian goose was sauce for the Augustinian gander.

Augustine saw God as absolute, transcendent and changeless.
On these, and similar, metaphysical assumptions he based his
theology. Working with such assumptions it was difficult to bring
God into relationship with the life of man because he was working with two modes of being which are heterogeneous. The
distance between God and man hovers over all Augustine's work.
It is seen in the strains within his theology of creation and the
sacraments. It is seen in individual terms in his spirituality and
in corporate terms in the *City of God*. The view of Hartshorne
represents the reaction of the modern temper: 'In Augustine's
discussion of God as the eternal Truth . . . the attitude is very
Greek; but what is its relation to the Gospels, the God of which
seems to respond rather to persons as a person. . .? The bland
identification of God with the absolute or the infinite today
appears to many of us as a species of idolatry.'[4] Not all our contemporaries would take this position, but it focuses one element in
the unease we have with Augustine.

No doubt one can make many adjustments to Augustine's
theology—correcting him, using broader resources than were
available to him. Dietrich Ritschl, for example, makes a critical
appraisal of Augustine's theology and suggests, particularly with
reference to Christology, some of the inadequacies that could be
rectified by an injection of Eastern Christian theology.[5] But
something more radical than this is required.

In the field of astrophysics for many years the attempt to create
models of the universe has been based upon certain metaphysical
assumptions. One of these has been the assumption that the 'red-
shift' in the spectra of light received from bodies moving away
from the observer, is consistent throughout the universe. Recent
observation of radio-sources has made it difficult to create coherent models as long as this assumption continues to be made. Just

as Einstein changed the assumptions of Newtonian physics, so
the next step forward in understanding the universe is likely to
come when new assumptions are postulated that can make sense
of the complex data now available. A similar metaphysical
change seems to be necessary if theology is to catch up with
changes in the patterns of thinking in the modern world. Many
of our present assumptions are due to the influence of the
assumptions within Augustine's theology. Williams has shown
how some of the problems we find in Augustine may be dealt
with by process theology, in which some fundamental changes
in metaphysics are involved.[6] Further work in this direction is
obviously important.

When we create our theological symbols are we ever describing something 'wholly other'? The dichotomy is not between
the rational and the non-rational, but the rational and the pre-
rational. Our symbols make discussable certain pre-rational
perceptions of 'the perfect' and associate them with our life in
this world. When we talk in the polarities of God and man we
are drawing from an experience of being men in which God is
already present. It would seem from the whole tenor of
Augustine's writings that this is where he really begins. When he
created symbols in which to express his understanding, he was
compelled by his time to choose categories that heightened the
polarity. Inevitably as we engage in the same enterprise we shall
have to use contemporary categories, but there seems a good
chance that we can avoid the polarization. As with Augustine,
any statements we succeed in making will only be provisional—
a stage in the continuum of theological exploration. This is a
task beyond the scope of this book and, in any case, is an ongoing
process to which the whole theological enterprise must address
itself.[7]

NOTES

1 B. Lonergan, *Method in Theology* (London, 1972) 24
2 Exodus 3 : 22. De doct. chr. II xl 60; 75
3 The literature about the early influence of Neoplatonism on
  Augustine is described by J. O'Meara in his introduction to *St
  Augustine Against the Academics* ACW 12, 19f.; cf. J. O'Meara,
  The Young Augustine (London, 1954) 131f.

4 C. Hartshorne, *Creative Synthesis and Philosophic Method* (London, 1970) 45

5 *Memory and Hope* (New York, 1967)

6 op. cit., 90f.

7 I am indebted, in a way that may not be apparent, to D. S. Browning's *Atonement and Personality* (Philadelphia, 1966) for some ideas that stimulated this paragraph.

BIBLIOGRAPHY

Aland, K. and Cross, F. L. (eds) *Studia Patristica* (Berlin, 1957f.)

Altaner, B. *Patrology* (Edinburgh-London, 1960)

Altizer, T. J. J. and Hamilton, W. *Radical Theology and the Death of God* (London, 1965)

Angus, S. *The Sources of the First Ten Books of Augustine's De Civitate Dei* (Princeton, 1906)

Arbesmann, R. 'Christ the Medicus humilis in St Augustine' in *Augustinus Magister*, Communications I (Paris, 1954)

Aristotle. *Rhetoric*, Loeb 193 (London, 1926)

Armstrong, A. H. 'Spiritual or intelligible Matter in Plotinus and St Augustine' in *Augustinus Magister*, Communications I (Paris, 1954)

Armstrong, A. H. and Markus, R. A. *Christian Faith and Greek Philosophy* (London, 1960)

Bailey, D. S. *The Man-Woman Relation in Christian Thought* (London, 1959)

Baldwin, C. S. in *The Province of Rhetoric*, ed. J. S. Schwartz and J. A. Rycenga (New York, 1965)

Barrow, R. H. *An Introduction to St Augustine's The City of God* (London, 1950)

Barth, K. *Church Dogmatics* (Edinburgh, 1936f.)

Battenhouse, R. W. (ed.) *A Companion to the Study of St Augustine* (New York, 1955)

Baynes, N. H. 'Eusebius and the Christian Empire' in *Byzantine Studies and Other Essays* (London, 1955)

—— 'The Political Ideas of St Augustine's De Civitate Dei' in *Byzantine Studies and Other Essays* (London, 1955)

Bell, C. and Newby, H. *Community Studies* (London, 1971)

Blakeney, E. H. *Lactantius' Epitome of the Divine Institutes* (London, 1950)

Bornkamm, G. 'musterion' in *Theological Dictionary of the New Testament*, ed. G. Kittel (Michigan, 1967)

Bonner, G. *St Augustine of Hippo* (London, 1960)

Bourke, V. J. *Augustine's Quest of Wisdom* (Milwaukee, 1945)
Boyer, C. in *Spirituality through the Centuries*, ed. J. Walsh (London, n.d.)
Brookes, E. H. *The City of God and the Politics of Crisis* (Oxford, 1960)
Brown, P. *Augustine of Hippo: a biography* (London, 1967) (Augustine)
—— *Religion and Society in the Age of Augustine* (London, 1972) (Religion and Society)
—— *The World of Late Antiquity* (London, 1971)
Browning, D. S. *Atonement and Personality* (Philadelphia, 1966)
Burleigh, J. H. S. 'Great Preachers—XIX: St Augustine' in *Theology*, September 1952
—— *The City of God. A Study of St Augustine's Philosophy* (London, 1949)
Burnaby, J. *Amor Dei. A Study of the Religion of St Augustine* (London, 1938)
Callahan, J. F. 'Basil of Caesarea: A new source of St Augustine's theory of time' in *Harvard Studies in Classical Philology* 63, 1958
—— *Four Views of Time in Ancient Philosophy* (Harvard, 1948)
Carré, M. H. *Realists and Nominalists* (Oxford, 1946)
Casserley, J. V. L. *The Christian in Philosophy* (London, 1949)
Chadwick, H. *Alexandrian Christianity*, LCC 2 (London, 1954)
—— *Origen: Contra Celsum* (Oxford, 1953) (Contra Celsum)
Clark, M. T. *Augustine, Philosopher of Freedom* (New York, 1958)
Cochrane, C. N. *Christianity and Classical Culture* (Oxford, 1940)
Copleston, F. *A History of Philosophy* (London, 1946)
Corbett, E. P. J. *Classical Rhetoric for the Modern Student* (New York, 1965)
Cox, H. *The Feast of Fools* (Cambridge, Mass., 1969)
—— *The Secular City* (London, 1965)
Cranz, F. E. 'De Civitate Dei XV 2, and Augustine's Idea of the Christian Society' in *Speculum* XXV, April 1950
—— 'The Development of Augustine's Ideas of Society before the Donatist Controversy' in *Harvard Theological Review* XLVII, October 1954

Davies, J. G. *Every Day God* (London, 1973)

Dawson, C. 'St Augustine and his Age' in *A Monument to St Augustine* (London, 1945)

Deane, H. A. *The Political and Social Ideas of St Augustine* (New York, 1966)

Dittes, J. E. 'Continuities between the life and thought of Augustine' in *Journal for the Scientific Study of Religion*, Fall 1965

Dix, G. *The Shape of the Liturgy* (London, 1945)

Dodd, C. H. *The Interpretation of the Fourth Gospel* (Cambridge, 1953)

Donna, R. B. *Despair and Hope. A study in Langland and Augustine* (Washington, 1948)

Drewery, B. *Origen and the Doctrine of Grace* (London, 1960)

Dudden, F. H. *The Life and Times of St Ambrose* (Oxford, 1935)

Dugmore, C. W. 'Sacrament and Sacrifice in the Early Fathers' in *Journal of Ecclesiastical History*, II, 1951

Eigkenboom, P. 'Christus Redemptor in the Sermons of St Augustine' in *Melanges offerts à Mlle Christine Mohrmann* (Utrecht/Anvers, 1963)

Fairweather, E. R. 'St Augustine's Interpretation of Infant Baptism' in *Augustinus Magister*, Communications II (Paris, 1954)

Feret, H.-M. 'Sacramentum-Res' in *Revue des sciences philosophie et théologie*, 29, 1940.

Ferguson, J. *Pelagius* (Cambridge, 1956)

Figgis, J. N. *The Political Aspects of St Augustine's 'City of God'* (London, 1921)

Flew, R. N. *The Idea of Perfection* (Oxford, 1934)

Florovsky, G. 'Eschatology in the Patristic Age' in *Studia Patristica*, II, 1957

—— 'The Concept of Creation in Saint Athansius' in *Studia Patristica*, VI, 1962

Frank, E. *Philosophical Understanding and Religious Truth* (Oxford, 1954)

Frankl, V. E. *The Doctor and the Soul. An Introduction to Logotherapy* (New York, 1955)

Frend, W. H. C. *The Donatist Church* (Oxford, 1952)

Gilson, E. 'Foreword' in *St Augustine The City of God*, ed.
V. J. Bourke (New York, 1958)
—— *The Christian Philosophy of St Augustine* (London, 1961)
Grabowski, S. J. *The Church. An Introduction to the Theology
of St Augustine* (St Louis, 1957)
Grant, R. M. *Miracle and Natural Law* (Amsterdam, 1952)
Green, W. B. 'St Augustine on Time' in *Scottish Journal of
Theology*, June 1965
Hanson, R. P. C. 'The Reaction of the Church to the Collapse
of the Western Roman Empire in the Fifth Century' in
Vigiliae Christianae, 26, December 1972
Haring, N. M. 'St Augustine's Use of the Word *Character*' in
Mediaeval Studies, XIV, 1952
Hartshorne, C. *Creative Synthesis and Philosophic Method*
(London, 1970)
Heiler, F. *Prayer* (New York, 1958)
Hebert, A. G. *Liturgy and Society* (London, 1935)
Hick, J. 'Evil' in *The Encyclopedia of Philosophy*, 3 (London,
1967)
Hill, E. 'St Augustine as a Preacher' in *Blackfriars*, 35, 1954
Hoare, F. R. *The Western Fathers* (London, 1954)
Hodgson, L. 'Christian Citizenship. Some reflections on St
Augustine, Ep. 138' in *Church Quarterly Review*, October–
December 1947
Howie, G. *Educational Theory and Practice in St Augustine*
(London, 1969)
Insko, C. A. and Schopeler, J. in *Attitudes and Behaviour*, ed.
K. Thomas (London, 1971)
Jaeger, W. *Paideia. The Ideals of Greek Culture* (Oxford, 1947)
Jordan, R. 'Time and Contingency in St Augustine' in *The
Review of Metaphysics*, 8, 1954–5
Jung, C. G. *Modern Man in Search of a Soul* (London, 1961)
Kellett, B. H. 'Time and Eternity' in *The Church Quarterly*,
April 1971
Kelly, J. N. D. *Early Christian Creeds* (London, 1950)
—— *Early Christian Doctrines* (London, 1958)
Kelvin, P. *The Bases of Social Behaviour* (London, n.d.)
Kierkegaard, S. *Concluding Unscientific Postscript* (Princeton,
1941)

Kirk, K. E. *The Vision of God* (London, 1931)

Krook, D. *Three Traditions of Moral Thought* (Cambridge, 1959)

Lacey, T. A. *Nature, Miracle and Sin* (London, 1916)

Lacour, L. L. 'If Aristotle Could Hear You Preach' in *Pastoral Psychology*, October 1965

Ladner, G. B. 'St Augustine's Conception of the Reformation of Man after the Image of God' in *Augustinus Magister*, Communications I (Paris, 1954) (Reformation)

—— 'St Gregory of Nyssa and St Augustine on the symbolism of the Cross' in *Late Classical and Medieval Studies in Honor of A. M. Friend*, ed. K. Weitzmann (Princeton, 1955)

—— *The Idea of Reform* (Harvard, 1959) (Idea of Reform)

Lauras, A. and Rondet, H. 'Le Thème des Deux Cités dans l'oeuvre de Saint Augustin' in *Études Augustiniennes* (Paris, 1953)

Lawson, J. *The Biblical Theology of St Irenaeus* (London, 1948)

Lonergan, B. *Method in Theology* (London, 1972)

Lyttkens, H. 'The Analogy between God and the World' in *Uppsala Universitets Årsskrift*, 1, 1953

Mackenzie, J. S. 'Notes on the Problem of Time' in *Mind*, 1912

Markus, R. A. 'Marius Victorinus and Augustine' in *The Cambridge History of Later Greek and Early Medieval Philosophy*, ed. A. H. Armstrong (Cambridge, 1967) (Cambridge History)

—— *Saeculum: History and Society in the Theology of St Augustine* (Cambridge, 1970) (Saeculum)

—— 'St Augustine on Signs' in *Phronesis*, II, 1957 (Signs)

—— 'The Roman Empire in Early Christian Historiography' in *The Downside Review*, October 1963

Marrou, H. I. 'Civitas Dei, civitas terrena: num tertium quid?' in *Studia Patristica*, II, 1957

—— *St Augustine and his influence through the ages* (London, 1957) (Influence)

—— *Saint Augustin et la culture antique* (Paris, 1938)

Marsden, D. *The Philosophy of Time* (Oxford, 1955)

Maurice, F. D. *The Friendship of Books and other lectures* (London, 1893)

Milford, T. R. *Foolishness to the Greeks* (London, 1953)

Miller, S. H. *The Dilemma of Modern Belief* (London, 1964)

Moltmann, J. *Theology of Hope* (London, 1967)

Mommsen, T. E. 'St Augustine and the Christian Idea of Progress' in *Journal of the History of Ideas*, XII, June 1951

Nygren, A. *Agape and Eros* (London, 1953)

O'Meara, J. 'Augustine the Artist and the Aeniad' in *Melanges offerts à Mlle Christine Mohrmann* (Utrecht/Anvers, 1963) (Augustine the Artist)

—— *Charter of Christendom: The Significance of the City of God* (New York, 1961)

—— *The Young Augustine* (London, 1954)

Ottley, R. L. *Studies in the Confessions of St Augustine* (London, 1919)

Pailin, D. A. 'A Christian Possibility of Proclaiming the "Death of God"' in *The Church Quarterly*, January 1969

Parry, J. *The Psychology of Human Communication* (London, 1967)

Pellegrino, M. *The True Priest* (Langley, 1968)

Pickman, E. M. *The Mind of Latin Christendom* (Oxford, 1937)

Polman, A. D. R. *The Word of God according to St Augustine* (London, 1961)

Pontet, M. *L'Exégèse de S Augustin Prédicateur* (Aubier, 1945)

Pope, H. *St Augustine of Hippo* (New York, 1961)

Portalié, E. *A Guide to the Thought of St Augustine* (London, 1960)

Pourrat, P. *Christian Spirituality* (London, 1922)

Prenter, R. 'Metaphysics and Eschatology in the Sacramental Teaching of St Augustine' in *Studia Theologica*, I 1–2, 1948

Przywara, E. *An Augustine Synthesis* (London, 1945)

Rahner, K. *Theological Investigations* (London, 1961f.)

Ramsey, I. T. *Religious Language* (London, 1957)

Rau, C. 'Theories of Time in Ancient Philosophy' in *The Philosophical Review*, 62, 1953

Ritschl, D. *Memory and Hope* (New York, 1967)

Rowe, T. T. 'Comparative Study of Spirituality' in *The London Quarterly and Holborn Review*, January 1966

—— 'Their Word to Our Day: II St Augustine of Hippo' in *Expository Times*, November 1968 (St Augustine)

Rowley, H. H. *Darius the Mede and the Four World Empires in the Book of Daniel* (Cardiff, 1959)

Rupp, E. G. *Patterns of Reformation* (London, 1969)
—— *The Righteousness of God* (London, 1953)
Schillebeeckx, E. *Christ the Sacrament* (London, 1971)
Scott, W. (ed.) *Hermetica* (Oxford, 1924)
Searle, J. *Verses from St Augustine* (London, 1953)
Srawley, J. H. *St Ambrose on the Sacrament and on the Mysteries* (London, 1950)
Suter, R. 'Augustine on Time, with some criticisms from Wittgenstein' in *Revue Internationale de Philosophie*, 16, 1962
TeSelle, E. *Augustine the Theologian* (London, 1970)
Thonssen, L. and Baird, A. C. *Speech Criticism* (New York, 1948)
Tinsley, E. J. 'Parable, Allegory and Mysticism' in *Vindications*, ed. A. Hanson (London, 1966)
—— *The Imitation of God in Christ* (London, 1960)
Unamuno, M. de *The Tragic Sense of Life* (London, 1962)
Van Bavel, T. *Répertoire Bibliographique de S Augustin* (Steenbrugis, 1963)
Van Der Meer, F. *Augustine the Bishop* (London, 1961)
—— 'Sacramentum chez St Augustin' in *La Maison-Dieu*, 13, 1948
Vidler, A. R. *The Theology of F. D. Maurice* (London, 1948)
Wainwright, G. *Eucharist and Eschatology* (London, 1971)
Watkin, E. I. in *A Monument to St Augustine* (London, 1945)
Whitaker, E. C. *Documents of the Baptismal Liturgy* (London, 1960)
Wiles, M. *The Making of Christian Doctrine* (Cambridge, 1967)
Williams, D. D. *The Spirit and the Forms of Love* (London, 1968)
Willis, G. G. *St Augustine and the Donatist Controversy* (London, 1950)
Wolfson, H. A. *Philo* (Harvard, 1947)
Woollcott, P. 'Some Considerations of Creativity and Religious Experience in St Augustine of Hippo' in *Journal for the Scientific Study of Religion*, Spring 1966
Yarnold, G. D. *The Moving Image* (London, 1966)

INDEX